ISSUES THAT CONCERN YOU

Risky Teen Behavior

Heidi Watkins, *Book Editor*

GREENHAVEN PRESS
A part of Gale, Cengage Learning

GALE
CENGAGE Learning·

Detroit • New York • San Francisco • New Haven, Conn • Waterville, Maine • London

Elizabeth Des Chenes, *Managing Editor*

© 2012 Greenhaven Press, a part of Gale, Cengage Learning

Gale and Greenhaven Press are registered trademarks used herein under license.

For more information, contact:
Greenhaven Press
27500 Drake Rd.
Farmington Hills, MI 48331-3535
Or you can visit our Internet site at gale.cengage.com

For product information and technology assistance, contact us at

Gale Customer Support, 1-800-877-4253
For permission to use material from this text or product, submit all requests online at www.cengage.com/permissions

Further permissions questions can be e-mailed to permissionrequest@cengage.com

Articles in Greenhaven Press anthologies are often edited for length to meet page requirements. In addition, original titles of these works are changed to clearly present the main thesis and to explicitly indicate the author's opinion. Every effort is made to ensure that Greenhaven Press accurately reflects the original intent of the authors. Every effort has been made to trace the owners of copyrighted material.

Cover image © George Fairbairn/Shutterstock.com.

LIBRARY OF CONGRESS CATALOGING-IN-PUBLICATION DATA

Risky teen behavior / Heidi Watkins, book editor.
   p. cm. -- (Issues that concern you)
  Includes bibliographical references and index.
  ISBN 978-0-7377-5698-2 (hardcover)
 1. Teenagers. 2. Risk-taking (Psychology) 3. Adolescent psychology. I. Watkins, Heidi.
  HQ796.R57 2012
  155.5--dc23

                                                2011035522

Printed in the United States of America
1 2 3 4 5 6 7 16 15 14 13 12

CONTENTS

"One night, heart thumping, she took her phone into the family bathroom, took off her clothes, aimed the phone's camera at the mirror and took a picture of herself from the neck down. Seconds later she pressed 'send' and the picture was his."[1]

In this account, Zoey (not her real name), a seventh grader, sends her picture to a slightly older boy. She does like him, or maybe rather *did* like him until the flirtatious texting became incessant requests for a nude photo. As most of these stories end, the boy passes the picture around, classmates start to stare as they walk by, and Zoey is left with regrets and with more boys texting her night and day asking her for more photos.

Sexting is obviously a risky behavior. You only have to think that it is a good idea for a split second, and once the text message, photo, or video is sent, there's no taking it back. While teens are well known for their risky behavior, sexting is one area that illustrates that teens are not the only risk takers these days. Whether involving videos, photos or merely words, notorious sexting cases like those of New York congressman Anthony Weiner and golfer Tiger Woods have taken over national newscasts for weeks. More recently (in July 2011), tabloids have rumored that *To Catch a Predator* reporter, Chris Hansen, is guilty of sending nearly nude pictures of himself to another reporter with whom he was having an affair. Lesser-known scandals are plentiful and make the local news for their criminal nature. Recent headlines alone include "Indiana Amish Man Charged in Sexting a 12-Year-Old After Driving Horse and Buggy to Police Sting"[2] (June 21, 2011); "Oklahoma Pastor Arrested Accused of 'Sexting' Teen"[3] (July 8, 2011); and "Sexting: Buffalo Law Enforcement Officer Charged"[4] (July 9, 2011).

Sexting, however, is not the only risky behavior for which teens are notorious but by no means alone. Unplanned pregnancy, illicit drug use, and drunk driving are just three other areas where adults are often not setting much of an example.

Some teens engage in the risky behavior of sexting. Adults who do so may jeopardize their careers. US Congressman Anthony Weiner was forced to resign due to sexting.

As a fifteen-year-old sophomore in high school, Kortesha Jones was the starting center on her high school basketball team, busy with her church and social life, and making above average grades. But like too many other teenage girls, Kortesha became pregnant. Her then boyfriend and the father of her child, however, was an adult. While this last part might seem surprising, it should not. In fact, according to The National Campaign to Prevent Teen and Unplanned Pregnancy, 52 percent of teen pregnancies are fathered by men at least three years older than the teen mother. Furthermore, an estimated two-thirds of the fathers are not teens at all, but are twenty years old or older.

Another fact that may be surprising, considering the amount of research and press surrounding teen pregnancy, is that school-age girls like Kortesha make up only a small percentage of unplanned pregnancies. Eighteen- and nineteen-year-olds are three times as likely as sixteen- to seventeen-year-olds to become pregnant: twenty-two per thousand versus seventy-four per thousand. Additionally, unmarried women in their twenties account for the majority of single mothers. Seven of ten pregnancies of women in their twenties are unplanned, according to The National Campaign to Prevent Teen and Unplanned Pregnancy.

Teens are also far from the only illegal drug users. According to the 2009 National Survey on Drug Use and Health, while eighteen- to twenty-year-olds represented the largest group of people that used an illicit drug within a month prior to the survey (22.2 percent), some older groups were not far behind and even outnumbered some teen groups. Twenty-one- to twenty-five-year-olds (20.5 percent) outpaced sixteen- to seventeen-year-olds (16.7 percent). Both the twenty-six- to twenty-nine-year-old (14.4 percent) and the thirty- to thirty-four-year-old (10.5 percent) age ranges outpaced thirteen- to fourteen-year-olds (9 percent). Furthermore, while most groups and all teen groups reported a higher percentage of illicit drug use for 2009 than for 2008, the most significant increase was among fifty- to fifty-four-year-olds.

Teens are not the only drunk drivers either. According to the US Census Bureau's *2011 Statistical Abstract*, in 2008, twenty-one- to twenty-four-year-old drivers involved in fatal car accidents were almost twice as likely as sixteen- to twenty-year-olds to have been intoxicated, 34.4 percent to 17.4 percent, respectively. In fact, twenty-five- to thirty-four-year-olds (30.8 percent), thirty-five- to forty-four-year-olds (25.3 percent), and forty-five- to fifty-four-year-olds (20.7 percent) were all more likely than sixteen- to twenty-year-olds to have had a blood alcohol content of .08 percent or greater if they were the driver in a fatal traffic accident. The only groups that did not outpace sixteen- to twenty-year-olds in this regard included those aged fifty-five and above.

Even though teens are not the only ones taking risks, risky teen behavior is definitely a matter worthy of discussion by professionals as well as by today's teens. The articles in this volume represent multiple viewpoints surrounding the issue. In addition, the volume contains two appendixes to help the reader understand the topic, as well as a thorough bibliography and a list of organizations to contact for further information. The appendix titled "What You Should Know About Risky Teen Behavior" offers vital facts about pregnancy and other risky behavior and how it affects young people. The appendix "What You Should Do About Risky Teen Behavior" offers information for young people confronted with this issue. With all these features, *Issues That Concern You: Risky Teen Behavior* is an excellent resource on this important topic.

Notes

1. Nicole Brady, "Scourge of the School Yard: How One Rash Moment Can Ruin a Young Life," *Age*, July 10, 2011. www .theage.com.au/victoria/scourge-of-the-school-yard-how-one-rash-moment-can-ruin-a-young-life-20110709-1h84z.html.
2. Reshma Kirpalani, "Indiana Amish Man Charged in Sexting a 12-Year-Old After Driving Horse and Buggy to Police Sting," ABC News, June 21, 2011. http://abcnews.go.com /US/indiana-amish-man-chareed-sexting-12-year-driving /story?id=13894438.
3. *Oklahoma City News*, "Oklahoma City Pastor Arrested, Accused of 'Sexting' Teen," July 8, 2011. www.koco.com /news/28484951/detail.html.
4. Melissa Linton, "Sexting: Buffalo Law Enforcement Officer Charged," *Buffalo True Crime Examiner*, July 9, 2011. www .examiner.com/true-crime-in-buffalo/sexting-buffalo-law-enforcement-officer-charged.

ONE

Risky Teen Behavior Is a Serious Problem

Centers for Disease Control and Prevention

> Every other year thousands of high school students par-
> ticipate in the Youth Risk Behavior Survey (YRBS) con-
> ducted by the Centers for Disease Control and Prevention
> (CDC), a federal agency of the US Department of Health
> and Human Services. For the 2009 survey, over sixteen
> thousand students from 158 schools shared their experi-
> ences. The complete results—over 140 pages—were pre-
> sented in the June 4, 2010, issue of *Morbidity and Mortality
> Weekly Report*. This viewpoint summarizes that report.
> Both are available on the CDC's Healthy Youth website
> along with many other publications presenting informa-
> tion from the YRBS and the Middle School YRBS as well
> as Youth Online, an interactive tool that produces custom
> graphs and tables.

The national Youth Risk Behavior Survey (YRBS) monitors six categories of priority health-risk behaviors among
youth and young adults, including behaviors that contribute
to unintentional injuries and violence; tobacco use; alcohol
and other drug use; sexual behaviors that contribute to unin-
tended pregnancy and sexually transmitted diseases (STDs),

including human immunodeficiency virus (HIV) infection; unhealthy dietary behaviors; and physical inactivity. In addition, the national YRBS monitors the prevalence of obesity and asthma. The national YRBS is conducted every two years during the spring semester and provides data representative of 9th- through 12th-grade students in public and private schools in the United States.

Behaviors That Contribute to Unintentional Injury and Violence

- 9.7% of students had rarely or never wore a seat belt when riding in a car driven by someone else.
- Among the 69.5% of students who had ridden a bicycle during the 12 months before the survey, 84.7% had rarely or never worn a bicycle helmet.
- 28.3% of students rode in a car or other vehicle driven by someone who had been drinking alcohol one or more times during the 30 days before the survey.
- 9.7% of students had driven a car or other vehicle one or more times when they had been drinking alcohol during the 30 days before the survey.
- 17.5% of students had carried a weapon, (e.g., a gun, knife, or club) on at least 1 day during the 30 days before the survey.
- 5.9% of students had carried a gun on at least 1 day during the 30 days before the survey.
- 31.5% of students had been in a physical fight one or more times during the 12 months before the survey.
- 5.6% of students had carried a weapon (e.g., a gun, knife, or club) on school property on at least 1 day during the 30 days before the survey.
- 7.7% of students had been threatened or injured with a weapon (e.g., a gun, knife, or club) on school property one or more times during the 12 months before the survey.
- 19.9% of students had been bullied on school property during the 12 months before the survey.

- 5.0% of students did not go to school because they felt they would be unsafe at school or on their way to or from school on at least 1 day during the 30 days before the survey.
- 13.8% of students had seriously considered attempting suicide and 6.3% of students had attempted suicide one or more times during the 12 months before the survey.

Two major components of risky behavior in teens are alcohol and drug abuse.

Tobacco Use

- 46.3% of students had ever tried cigarette smoking (even one or two puffs).
- 19.5% of students smoked cigarettes on at least 1 day during the 30 days before the survey.
- 8.9% of students had used smokeless tobacco (e.g., chewing tobacco, snuff, or dip) on at least 1 day during the 30 days before the survey.
- 5.1% of students had smoked cigarettes on school property on at least 1 day during the 30 days before the survey.

Alcohol and Other Drug Use

- 72.5% of students had had at least one drink of alcohol on at least 1 day during their life and 41.8% of students had had at least one drink of alcohol on at least 1 day during the 30 days before the survey.
- 4.5% of students had drunk at least one drink of alcohol on school property on at least 1 day during the 30 days before the survey.
- 24.2% of students had had five or more drinks of alcohol in a row (i.e., within a couple of hours) on at least 1 day during the 30 days before the survey.
- 36.8% of students had used marijuana one or more times during their life.
- 20.8% of students had used marijuana one or more times during the 30 days before the survey.
- 2.8% of students had used any form of cocaine (e.g., powder, crack, or freebase) one or more times during the 30 days before the survey.
- 11.7% of students had ever sniffed glue, breathed the contents of aerosol spray cans, or inhaled any paints or sprays to get high one or more times during their life.
- 4.1% of students had used methamphetamines (also called "speed", "crystal", "crank", or "ice") one or more times during their life.
- 3.3% of students had taken steroid pills or shots without a doctor's prescription one or more times during their life.

Many Teens Engage in Risky Behavior

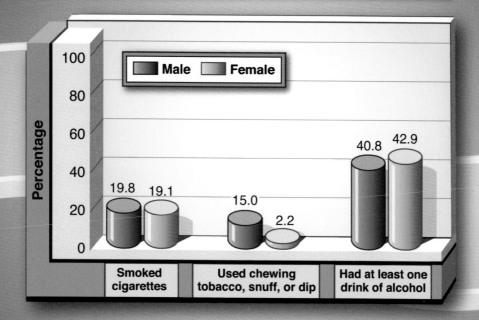

Percentage of students who smoked cigarettes; used chewing tobacco, snuff, or dip; or had at least one drink of alcohol on at least one day during the 30 days before the survey, by sex:

Taken from: Centers for Disease Control and Prevention, "2009 Youth Risk Behavior Survey Overview," June 4, 2010.

Sexual Behaviors That Lead to Pregnancy and Diseases

- 46.0% of students had ever had sexual intercourse.
- 13.8% of students had had sexual intercourse with four or more persons during their life.
- 34.2% of students had had sexual intercourse with at least one person during the 3 months before the survey.
- Among the 34.2% of currently sexually active students, 61.1% reported that either they or their partner had used a condom during last sexual intercourse.

- Among the 34.2% of currently sexually active students, 22.9% reported that either they or their partner had used birth control pills or [the injectable contraceptive] Depo-Provera to prevent pregnancy before last intercourse.

Physical Activity
- 18.4% of students were physically active at least 60 minutes per day on each of the 7 days during the 7 days before the survey.
- 23.1% of students did not participate in at least 60 minutes of physical activity on at least 1 day during the 7 days before the survey.
- 24.9% of students played video or computer games or used a computer for something that was not school work for 3 or more hours per day on an average school day.
- 32.8% of students watched television 3 or more hours per day on an average school day.
- 56.4% of students attended physical education (PE) classes on 1 or more days in an average week when they were in school and 33.3% of students attended PE classes daily in an average week when they were in school.

Dietary Behaviors and Obesity
- 33.9% of students had eaten fruit or drank 100% fruit juices two or more times per day during the 7 days before the survey.
- 13.8% of students ate vegetables three or more times per day during the 7 days before the survey.
- 22.3% of students had eaten fruits and vegetables five or more times per day during the 7 days before the survey.
- 29.2% of students had drunk a can, bottle, or glass of soda or pop (not including diet soda or diet pop) at least one time per day during the 7 days before the survey.
- 12.0% of students were obese and 15.8% of students were overweight.
- 10.6% of students went without eating for 24 or more hours to lose weight or to keep from gaining weight during the 30 days before the survey.

- 5.0% of students took diet pills, powders, or liquids to lose weight or keep from gaining weight during the 30 days before the survey.
- 4.0% of students vomited or took laxatives to lose weight or to keep from gaining weight during the 30 days before the survey.

Other Health-Related Topics
- 22.0% of students had ever been told by a doctor or nurse that they had asthma and 10.8% of students still have asthma.
- 9.3% of students most of the time or always wore sunscreen with an SPF of 15 or higher when outside for more than 1 hour on a sunny day.
- 15.6% of students had used an indoor tanning device such as a sunlamp, sunbed, or tanning booth one or more times during the 12 months before the survey.
- 30.9% of students had 8 or more hours of sleep on an average school night.

TWO

Risky Teen Behaviors Have Declined

Kathleen Carroll and Leslie Brody

The Youth Risk Behavior Survey (YRBS) is conducted every two years by a division of the US Centers for Disease Control and Prevention (CDC). Results are available at the CDC's Healthy Youth website. Communities who participated can pull their results and compare them with results from other communities and with their own results from previous years. This viewpoint is just one example of information available from the YRBS. In it Kathleen Carroll and Leslie Brody, staff writers for the *Bergen County Record*, a newspaper in New Jersey, note declines in the risky behaviors of New Jersey teens, including drinking, smoking, and sexual activity. They also note gaps in the survey, however, since no questions regarding illegal use of prescription medications or suicide attempts were included in the YRBS years examined.

Half of high school students had tried smoking.

More than a third had tried marijuana.

One in 10 had recently been in a fistfight at school.

But overall, fewer New Jersey teenagers last year [in 2005] said they drank, smoked or had sex compared with teenagers five years ago, according to a biennial survey of high school students released Tuesday [October 3, 2006,] by the state Education Department.

"Young people are reporting less risky behaviors," acting Commissioner Lucille Davy said. "That is obviously a positive thing for us to note."

For the first time last year, New Jersey also conducted a survey of middle school students in Grades 7 and 8 that included questions on body image, smoking, drug use and suicide.

Twenty-three percent reported they had "seriously thought about killing themselves."

"Why kids at that age are thinking about suicide is something we ought to be concerned about," Davy said. Although the middle school survey was too small to be considered statistically significant, the suicide responses were worrisome, education officials said.

The data are from the voluntary 2005 Youth Risk Behavior Survey, which included questions on safety and violence, smoking, drug and alcohol use, sexual behavior, diet and exercise. The high school survey was given to 1,500 students at 29 public high schools last year.

Sex and Drinking Are Down

High school students reported they were having less sex and were more likely to use birth control than teenagers five years ago. About 44 percent said they had had sex, compared with 47 percent in 2001. About 71 percent said they had used a condom the last time they had sex, compared with 64 percent in the earlier survey.

Overall, fewer high school students said they were using alcohol. About 47 percent said they had had a drink in the past 30 days, compared with 56 percent five years ago. One-fifth of students said they had tried drinking before age 13, compared with one-third of students five years ago.

Surveys nationwide have shown declines in teenage drinking, but the level is "still unacceptable," and parents need to do more, said Alicia Poleshuk, education coordinator for the Bergen County Council on Alcoholism.

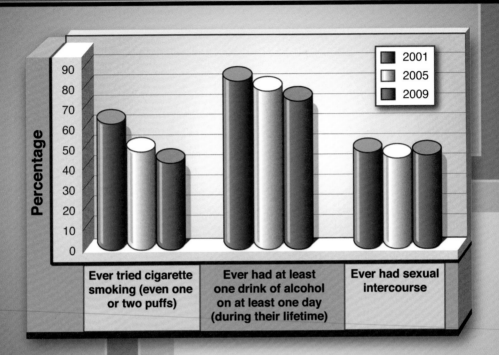

Percentage of New Jersey Teens Who Have Tried Smoking, Drinking, and Sex, 2001–2009

Legend: 2001, 2005, 2009

Y-axis: Percentage (0, 10, 20, 30, 40, 50, 60, 70, 80, 90)

Categories:
- Ever tried cigarette smoking (even one or two puffs)
- Ever had at least one drink of alcohol on at least one day (during their lifetime)
- Ever had sexual intercourse

Taken from: Centers for Disease Control and Prevention, Youth Online: "High School Risk Behavior Survey," New Jersey 2001–2009. http://apps.nccd.cdc.gov/youthonline.

Research shows that adolescents with strong ties to their families, schools or community institutions, such as a church or a sports team, are less likely to experiment with drugs or alcohol. Poleshuk suggested that parents talk frankly with their children about stress and alcohol use and examine their own behavior to see what examples they set at home.

"It takes a lot of introspection," she said. "Look at the message you're communicating. Is it OK to have adult parties and let people get loaded? Is it OK for my child to see me drinking and driving? Is it OK to have alcohol in the house?"

Prescription Drug Abuse Is on the Rise

Andy Yeager, a student assistance counselor at Park Ridge High School, said any decline in alcohol consumption may be explained partly by a rise in abuse of prescription drugs. The questionnaire did not ask students about such drug use.

"Prescription painkillers are easy to get, all over the place," he said. "With $5, you can get a pill without any problem at school."

About 33 percent of high school students reported being offered, sold or given an illegal drug on school property. But fewer students reported using cocaine or heroin, sniffing glue, injecting illegal drugs or taking methamphetamines than in 2001.

Students also reported less tobacco use than in previous years, after years of anti-smoking campaigns aimed at children.

Half of high school students said they had tried smoking, compared with almost two-thirds in 2001. One out of five students said they had smoked in the last month, compared with 30 percent five years ago.

In April, a new state law raised the minimum age to purchase cigarettes to 19 from 18.

"The smoking decrease is significant," Davy said. "Hopefully that's a sign that we've done some of the right things to help."

Suicide Not on the Survey

The high school survey did not include questions about suicide, which are included in the survey every few years, officials said. In the 2001 survey, 17 percent of high school students reported they had seriously considered suicide, down from 22 percent in 1995.

Among middle school students, almost twice the proportion of girls as boys said they had considered suicide: 28 percent versus 16 percent. About 30 percent of Hispanic students—and 37 percent of Hispanic girls—said they had considered suicide, compared with about 20 percent for white or African-American students. Eight percent of students said they had attempted suicide.

Females attempt suicide more often than males, but nationwide, males account for 80 percent of all fatalities, according to the federal Centers for Disease Control and Prevention. While

New Jersey has one of the lowest suicide rates in the nation, suicide is the third-leading cause of death for people ages 10 to 24. Nationwide, suicide rates among teenagers have tripled since the 1940s.

This summer [2006], the Education Department published guidelines for how schools should handle suspicion that a child may be suicidal. A law signed last January requires all public school teachers to have two hours of training in suicide prevention.

"It is a leading cause of death for young people in New Jersey," said Assemblyman Michael Panter, D-Monmouth, who sponsored the legislation. "Parents are often in the best position to recognize those signs. But aside from family members, teachers are really the adults who are in the most frequent contact with these kids."

Because prescription painkillers are easier to obtain than alcohol, abuse of such drugs is somewhat more common than alcohol abuse.

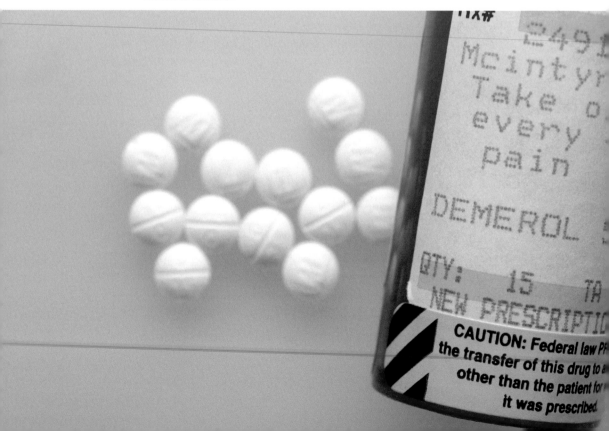

Movies and media reports feature stories of suicide, and so middle school students may be more likely to think of it when they are overwhelmed by homework, bullying or depression, said Steven Sussman, a child and adolescent psychologist in Mountainside.

"Kids are much more aware of the concept," he said. "Thirty years ago a kid would say, 'I want to run away.' Would they be more likely to commit suicide now? I can't say. Most kids before didn't really run away. It's sort of the new language of expressing how angry, hurt, despondent you are."

Teens Opening Up More

Adolescents are notoriously reluctant to talk about their problems. But that may be changing, said Gloria Leder, clinical director at Family Counseling Service in Ridgewood.

"It used to be they'd roll their eyes," she said. "[Now] they're aware that if they come here, they're here for a reason. . . . Five years ago, it was 'This is what I'm doing and don't you tell me not to. My mother's bringing me here, and what does she know?' Now they say, 'I hear you.' It seems like there's an awareness."

THREE

Teens Take Risks Because Their Brains Have Not Matured

Junior Scholastic

Scientists have been studying the human brain for hundreds of years. The study of the development of the human brain and the differences between teen and adult brains has been a special focus of more recent brain research. This article from *Junior Scholastic*, a newsmagazine for young teens, explains what scientists understand about the brain functions involved in decision-making processes and how those functions develop as brains mature. This research provides some answers for why decision-making processes are different for teens than for adults and suggests what teens can do to make smarter decisions.

Picture this: Your finger is poised on the *send* button, your eyes scanning an angry e-mail you've dashed off to a friend who has upset you. Some things you've written are a little harsh. In your brain a little red light goes off, but, what the heck, you're steamed and your friend deserves it. You push the button.

Whether you're aware or not, rushed decisions like this— acting before *thinking it through*—happen more often in teens than in adults. Recent discoveries in brain science may help explain why this is so.

First, a bit on how a brain makes decisions. Decisions don't "just happen" automatically in your conscious mind. They stem from a series of events in the brain, which happen almost instantaneously. This involves a relay system in which different structures—made up of specialized cells called neurons—talk with each other by way of electrochemical impulses and chemical messengers, called neurotransmitters. Information flowing through this decision-making circuit is analyzed in the different structures. Then the network, as a whole, puts out a response. This output provides the basis for our behaviors and actions.

While this process is basically the same for teens and adults, the devil is in the details. Since the brain is not fully developed until the early 20s, the way in which a teen's decision-making circuit integrates information may put him or her at a higher risk of making decisions the teen could later regret.

The Teen Brain: Under Construction

Not long ago, scientists thought the human brain was fully mature long before the teen years. While research shows that one's brain reaches its maximum size between ages 12 and 14 (depending on whether you are a girl or a boy), it also shows that brain development is far from complete. Regions of the brain continue to mature all the way through a person's early 20s.

A key brain region that matures late is the *prefrontal cortex*, located directly behind your forehead. The prefrontal cortex is very important as a control center for thinking ahead and sizing up risks and rewards. (This area is, in fact, the little red light that was trying to warn you about sending that e-mail.) Meanwhile, another part of the brain that matures earlier is the *limbic system*, which plays a central role in emotional responses.

Since the limbic system matures earlier, it is more likely to gain an upper hand in decision making. This relationship between the emotional center (limbic system) and control center (prefrontal cortex) helps to explain a teen's inclination to rush decisions. In other words, when teens make choices in emotionally charged situations, those choices are often more weighted in *feelings* (the mature limbic system) over *logic* (the not-yet-mature prefrontal cortex).

This is also why teens are more likely to make "bad" choices, such as using drugs, alcohol, and tobacco—all of which pose a risk of serious health consequences. "Most kids don't really 'plan' to use drugs," says Professor Laurence Steinberg of Temple University, "at least not the first time. They are more likely to experiment *on the spur of the moment*, particularly when influenced by others [peer pressure]."

Because their brains are not fully mature, teens who make choices in emotionally charged situations often bypass logic and may become involved in risky behavior.

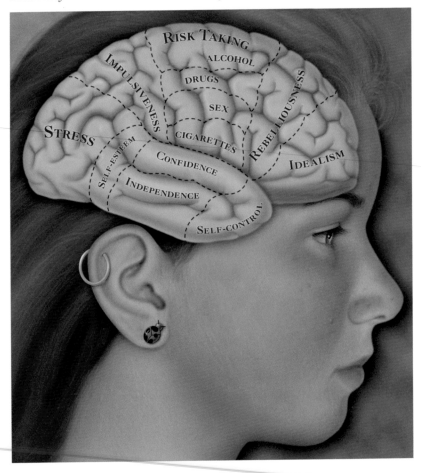

Fine-Tuning the Brain

Like the rest of the body, the brain needs to mature in order to reach peak performance. This process involves slow changes—strongly influenced by brain activity—that have evolved to fine-tune (or optimize) how neural impulses flow throughout the brain, allowing it to process information faster and more reliably.

Inside the brain, information travels through a network of neurons, which have thread-like fibers called *axons* and branch-like structures called *dendrites*. Dendrites bring information into the neurons, while axons take it away and pass it along to the next neuron. Thus, neurons are assembled into circuits where the far end of an axon (its terminal) is positioned close to a dendrite. The small space between the two is called a *synapse*—where information is exchanged.

Throughout childhood and adolescence, the brain is busy fine-tuning itself through two key processes: myelination and synaptic pruning. In *myelination*, axons wrap themselves in a fatty substance (myelin sheath), which works like the insulating plastic that surrounds electrical wires. This boosts the brain's efficiency by increasing the speed with which a signal travels down the axon by up to 100 times. In *synaptic pruning*, synapses not used very often are removed, allowing the brain to redirect precious resources toward more active synapses. This strategic loss of weak synapses shapes the brain and makes it more efficient. This important pruning process molds the brain in response to a person's experiences and activities.

This means that teens have the potential, through their choices and the behaviors they engage in, to shape their own brain development—strengthening some circuits and getting rid of others. This makes the type of activities teens are involved in especially important. Skill-building activities, such as many physical, learning, and creative endeavors, not only provide stimulating challenges, but can simultaneously build strong brain pathways. When teens learn and repeat appropriate behaviors, they are helping to shape their brains—and their futures.

How Information Travels in the Brain

A synapse is the small space where an axon and dendrite exchange information.

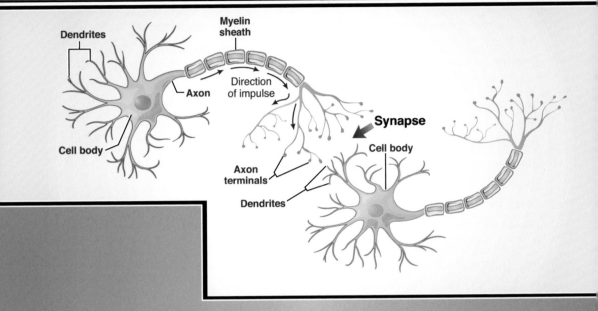

Taken from: *Junior Scholastic*, "Teens and Decision Making: What Brain Science Reveals," April 14, 2008. Copyright © 2008 by Scholastic Inc. All rights reserved. Reproduced by permission.

Wait Before Acting

Learning how your brain works can help explain why sometimes you behave like you do. With this knowledge, you can be better equipped to make smart choices.

One tip to follow is to *take a moment* before acting. When making a decision, something as simple as stopping to think can mean the difference between a positive and a negative outcome. By waiting a minute before acting, you allow yourself to:

- consider consequences;
- weigh harmful outcomes (e.g., harm to yourself or others) against short-term benefits (e.g., fitting in or feeling high);
- determine whether peer pressure is making you do something you'd otherwise not do;
- get information or advice, if you need it.

FOUR

Are Brains of Reckless Teens More Mature than Those of Their Prudent Peers?

Robert Epstein and Jennifer Ong

The prevailing theory for risky teen behavior has been that parts of the teenage brain have not finished developing—that teens take dangerous risks because their brains are not yet like adult brains. In this viewpoint writers and researchers Robert Epstein and Jennifer Ong explain research that indicates the opposite of prevailing theory—that the brains of teens who take risks are *more* like the brains of adults. The research, conducted by neuroscientists at Emory University, does not explain why, however, and the question is asked, do teens with adult-like brains take more risks or does taking risks make teen brains more adult-like?

Thrill seeking and poor judgment go hand in hand when it comes to teenagers—an inevitable part of human development determined by properties of a growing but immature brain. Right? Not so fast. A study [from August 16, 2009] turns that thinking upside down: The brains of teens who behave dangerously are more like adult brains than are those of their more cautious peers.

Psychologists have long believed that the brain's judgment-control systems develop more slowly than emotion-governing systems, not maturing until people are in their mid-20s. Hence, teens end up taking far more risks than adults do. Evidence supporting this idea comes from studies looking at functional and structural properties of gray matter, the important part of the brain that contains the neurons that relay brain signals.

At least two observations undermine this theory, however. First, American-style teen turmoil is absent in more than 100 cultures around the world, suggesting that such mayhem is not biologically inevitable. Second, the brain itself changes in response to experiences, raising the question of whether adolescent brain characteristics are the *cause* of teen tumult or rather the *result* of lifestyle and experiences. Because brain research is virtually always correlational in design, determining whether brain properties are causes or effects is impossible.

Now neuroscientists Gregory S. Berns, Sara Moore and Monica Capra of Emory University suggest that teen risk-taking is associated not with an immature brain but with a mature, adultlike brain—exactly the opposite of conventional wisdom.

Risk and White Matter

The researchers assessed 91 teens from ages 12 to 18 in two ways: First, teens completed the Adolescent Risk-Taking Questionnaire (ARQ), designed to measure their engagement in dangerous behaviors such as drinking, smoking, taking drugs, and having unprotected sex. Subjects were also screened for actual drug use, which was predicted well by test scores. Second, a technology known as diffusion tensor imaging (DTI) was used to assess the development of white matter in the frontal cortex of teens' brains. White matter consists of myelin, a fatty substance that coats the long axons, which carry brain signals; its main function is to increase the efficiency of neural signaling. Between childhood and adolescence, it grows in volume and becomes better organized, improving our ability to think and function.

This colored diffusion tensor imaging (DTI) scan shows bundles of white matter nerve fibers (in orange and green) in the brainstem. DTI has been used to assess the development of white matter in the frontal cortex of teen brains.

According to Berns, DTI technology takes advantage of the fact that water molecules tend to move along myelin pathways. In an immature brain, water throughout the brain diffuses in a roughly spherical, cloudlike pattern, but as the brain matures and myelin "tracts" form and grow around axons, water starts to move along those tracts in patterns that the imaging technique picks up as lines radiating throughout the brain.

If the existing theory about the teen brain is correct, then the higher the ARQ score, the less developed the white matter should be—but that is not what the Berns team discovered. "It was surprising," Berns says. "I assumed we'd find that risk-taking would be associated with an immature brain." In fact, he found the opposite—a strong positive correlation between engagement in dangerous behaviors and the increased myelination typical of mature brains. In other words, young people who engage in dangerous behaviors generally have a more adultlike brain than their conservative peers.

Against Conventional Wisdom

As for the conventional thinking about the teen brain, according to Berns, "after reviewing all of the neurodevelopment stuff, I couldn't really find any link between brain development and adolescent risk-

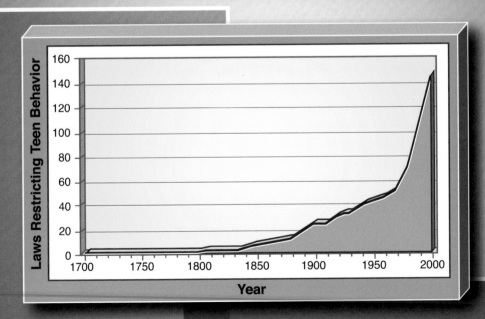

Laws Restricting Teen Behavior Have Increased

US teens have ten times as many restrictions as adults, twice as many as active-duty US Marines, and twice as many as incarcerated felons.

taking. Nobody denies that the brain develops or that teens take risks, but how the two got intertwined is beyond me." Nevertheless, the accepted view of the teen brain is so powerful, Berns says, that his paper faced a lengthy and tumultuous review process. . . .

If valid, the study has important implications for interpreting risk-taking in teens. It suggests that the brains of many teens who behave dangerously are maturing early: Reckless behavior might in fact be a sign of adultness. Some adults do risky things (speeding, drinking, having unprotected sex) quite commonly without causing great alarm. Automatically considering such behaviors to be more objectionable just because someone is young runs into what the researchers call in their paper "a conundrum of defining risk (or dangerousness) based not on the objective attributes of the activity but on the person engaging in them."

Room for Skepticism

Berns also acknowledges that the new study says nothing about causation, just like the gray matter studies. "Could someone whose brain develops earlier start to engage in adult activities earlier?" That is one possibility, he says, but it is also possible that "engaging in adult activities makes the brain mature faster," he says.

Not everyone thinks the new study will overturn thinking about the teenage brain. Developmental psychologist Laurence Steinberg of Temple University says he has been aware of the Berns research for several years and that it is flawed. "There are findings from other studies that in some respects contradict these findings," Steinberg says. "For instance, it's been shown that individuals with more developed white matter tracts are less oriented toward immediate rewards and less susceptible to peer pressure"— meaning they are probably less prone to risk-taking.

Michael S. Gazzaniga of the University of California, Santa Barbara, one of the pioneers in modern neuroscience, sees the Berns study more positively. The large number of subjects makes the results hard to ignore, he says, and they need to be taken seriously. Says Gazzaniga: "So much for the much touted model that the tumultuous teenage brain is that way because it is not fully developed. Back to the drawing board again."

FIVE

Taking Risks May Help Teens Develop Lifelong Skills

Nancy Shute

There is no question that teens are notorious risk takers. The question has always been why? In this viewpoint
journalist Nancy Shute, a senior writer for *US News &
World Report*, provides some answers. Shute discusses how,
beginning in the 1990s, medical technology has given scientists a better picture of the teen brain, enabling them for
the first time to understand why teens tend to take risks
and why addictions starting in the teen years are so devastating. She points out, however, that the neurological
state that explains teen addiction also explains the special
aptitude teens have for learning, and that the neurological
state that explains the propensity for teens to take risks
that might kill them is the same state that makes them
more likely to have and act on innovative ideas.

Behold the American teenager, a lump in a hoodie who's capable of little more than playing "Grand Theft Auto," raiding
the liquor cabinet, and denting the minivan, thanks to a brain
so unformed that it's more like a kindergartner's than a grown-
up's. That's the message that seemed to emerge from the past
decade's neuroscientific discoveries: that the brain, once thought
to be virtually complete by age 6, is very much a work in progress

during adolescence and *not* to be trusted. But experts now are realizing that the popular parental response—to coddle teens in an attempt to shield them from every harm—actually may be counterproductive.

Yes, teenagers make woefully errant decisions that factor big in the 13,000 adolescent deaths each year. And yes, their unfinished brains appear to be uniquely vulnerable to substance abuse and addiction. But they also are capable of feats of learning and daring marvelous enough to make a grown-up weep with jealousy. How they exercise these capabilities, it now appears, helps shape the brain wiring they'll have as adults. "You have this power you're given," says Wilkie Wilson, codirector of DukeLEARN, a new program at Duke University designed to teach teenagers how to best deploy their brains. Far from coddling the kids, he says, Mom and Dad need to figure out how to allow enough "good" risk-taking to promote growth and prevent wasted talent—while also avoiding disaster.

It can be a nerve-racking exercise. "These kids are such a crazy mix of impulsiveness and shrewdness," says Marcia Harrington, a survey researcher in Silver Spring, Md. She recalls the time she thought her then 16-year-old daughter, Alexandra Plante, had sleepover plans, but the girl instead ditched school and flew to Chicago to visit an acquaintance she'd met briefly during a family trip. The scheme was revealed only because bad weather delayed the flight home. Alex returned unharmed and has never conceded that the escapade was too risky. "She's going to be a great adult someday," says Harrington. "But, boy, there are moments that are terrifying." Further along the road to adulthood now, Alex has applied her daring spirit to becoming an emergency medical technician and volunteer for the local fire department, and to heading off to college 2,500 miles from home.

Taking a Peek Under the Hood

While society has known since forever that adolescents can be impulsive risk-takers, it wasn't until the 1990s, when MRI [magnetic resonance imaging] scans became a common research tool,

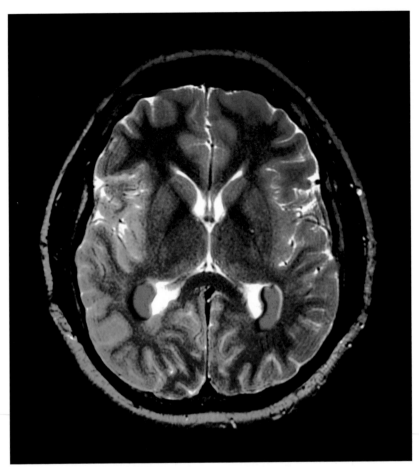

This cross-sectional magnetic resonance imaging brain scan shows developing gray matter in red. Gray matter grows gradually throughout childhood and peaks at around age twelve.

that scientists could peek into the teenage cranium and begin to sort out why. What they found astonished them. The brain's gray matter, which forms the bulk of its structure and processing capacity, grows gradually throughout childhood, peaks around age 12, and then furiously "prunes" underused neurons.

By scanning hundreds of children as they've grown up, neuroscientists at the National Institute of Mental Health [NIMH] have been able to show that the pruning starts at the back of the brain and moves forward during adolescence. Regions that control sensory and motor skills mature first, becoming more specialized and efficient. The prefrontal cortex, responsible for judgment and impulse control, matures last. Indeed, the prefrontal cortex isn't "done" until the early 20s—and sometimes even later in men. Meantime, the brain's white matter, which acts as the cabling connecting brain parts, becomes thicker and better able to transmit signals quickly. Recent research shows that this myelination process of white matter continues well past adolescence, perhaps even into middle age.

Now, dozens of researchers are studying how all these changes might affect adolescent behavior, and also shape adult skills and behavior, for good and for ill. The maturation lag between emotional and cognitive brain centers may help explain why teenagers get so easily upset when parents see no reason, for example; teens seem to process input differently than do adults.

In one experiment, young teenagers trying to read the emotions on people's faces used parts of the brain designed to quickly recognize fear and alarm; adults used the more rational prefrontal cortex. Deborah Yurgelun-Todd, the researcher at McLean Hospital in Belmont, Mass., who led this work, believes young teens are prone to read emotion into their interactions and miss content. Therefore, parents may have better luck communicating with middle-schoolers if they avoid raising their voice (easier said than done) and instead explain how they're feeling.

Other experiments shed light on why even book-smart teenagers come up short on judgment: Their brain parts aren't talking to each other. When Monique Ernst, a child psychiatrist and neurophysiologist at NIMH, uses functional MRI to watch teenage and adult brains engaged in playing a gambling game, she finds that the "reward" center lights up more in teens than in adults when players are winning, and the "avoidance" region is less activated in teens when they're losing. There's also less activity in teens' prefrontal cortex, which adults use to mediate the "yes!" and "no" impulses from other brain regions. "The hypothesis is that there is this triumvirate of brain regions that needs to be in balance" in order to produce wise judgments, says Ernst, whether that's to wear a seat belt or use contraception.

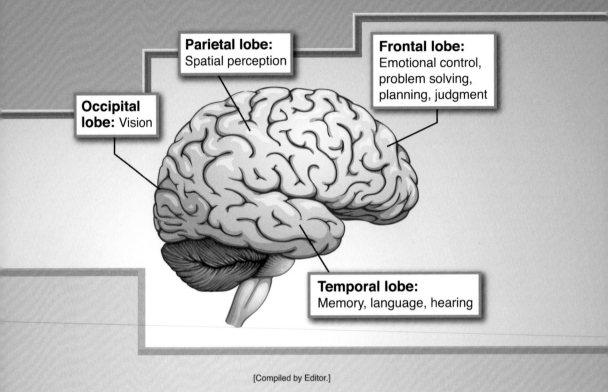

Lobes of the Brain

Studies by the National Institute of Mental Health have shown that the frontal lobe of the brain matures last.

Parietal lobe:
Spatial perception

Frontal lobe:
Emotional control, problem solving, planning, judgment

Occipital lobe: Vision

Temporal lobe:
Memory, language, hearing

[Compiled by Editor.]

Does an Unfinished Brain Make for Bad Behavior?

There is as yet no proven link between bright blobs on an MRI and real-life behavior, but researchers are hard at work trying to make that connection. In a 2005 study by Laurence Steinberg, a developmental psychologist at Temple University, teenagers in a simulated driving test were twice as likely to drive dangerously if they had two friends with them—and brain scans showed that the reward centers lit up more if teens were told that friends were watching. A savvy parent might conclude that what's needed in the teen years is more guidance, not less.

In fact, study after study has shown that one of the most powerful factors in preventing teenage pregnancy, crime, drug and alcohol abuse, and other seriously bad outcomes is remarkably simple: time with responsible adults. "It doesn't have to be parents, necessarily," says Valerie Reyna, a professor of psychology at Cornell University. But it does mean that teenagers should be directly monitored by responsible adults so they have less time to get in trouble. Reyna thinks adults also need to teach what she calls "gist" thinking, or the ability to quickly grasp the bottom line. Instead, she says, teenagers often overthink but miss the mark. When Reyna asks adults if they'd play Russian roulette for $1 million, they almost universally say no. Half of teenagers say yes. "They'll tell you with a straight face that there's a whole lot of money, and they're probably not going to die. It's very logical on one level, but on another level, it's completely insane."

If it's any comfort, the evidence suggests that teenagers' loopy behavior and combativeness is hard-wired to push them out of the nest. Adolescent primates, rodents, and birds also hang out with their peers and fight with their parents, notes B.J. Casey, a teen brain researcher who directs the Sackler Institute at Weill Medical College of Cornell University in New York City. "You need to take risks to leave your family and village and find a mate."

A Turbocharged Learning Machine

The revved-up adolescent brain is also built to learn, the new research shows—and those teen experiences are crucial. Neurons, like muscles, operate on a "use it or lose it" basis; a teenager who studies piano three hours a day will end up with different brain wiring than someone who spends that same time shooting hoops or playing video games. A 16-year-old who learns to treat his girlfriend with care and compassion may well develop different emotional brain triggers than one who's thinking just about the sex.

Only in early childhood, it turns out, are people as receptive to new information as they are in adolescence. The human brain is designed to pay attention to things that are new and different, a process called salience. Add in the fact that emotion and passion also heighten attention and tamp down fear, and teenagerhood turns out to be the perfect time to master new challenges. "You are the owners of a very special stage of your brain development," Frances Jensen, a neurologist at Children's Hospital Boston, tells teenagers in her "Teen Brain 101" lectures at local high schools. "You can do things now that will set you up later in life with an enhanced skill set. Don't waste this opportunity." (She was motivated to create the talks by her own befuddling experiences as a single mother of two teenage boys.)

Jordan Dickey is one teen who seized opportunity. As a 14-year-old high-school freshman, he asked his father for something unusual: a $26,000 loan to start a business. The Dickey family, of Ramer, Tenn., raised a few cattle, and Jordan had noticed that people paid a lot more for hay in square bales than for the same amount in less-convenient round bales. After doing a feasibility study as an agriculture class project, Jordan convinced his dad to give him a three-year loan to buy a rebaling machine. He worked nights and weekends, mowing, raking, and rebaling; paid friends $7 an hour to load the bales into a trailer; and hired drivers to deliver the hay to local feed marts, since he was too young to drive. "It taught me how to manage my own money," Jordan says.

That's an understatement. Not only did he pay off the loan in one year, he made an additional $40,000. Now 17 and a senior, he has saved enough money to pay for a big chunk of college, much to his parents' delight. "He likes for the job to get done and get done right," says Perry Dickey, who owns an electroplating shop. "It was a big responsibility for him, and I'm glad he took the lines and produced."

Teens can apply the new findings to learn more without more study, notes Wilson, whose DukeLEARN program will be tested in ninth-grade health classes next year [2009]. Key points:

- Brains need plenty of sleep because they consolidate memory during slumber.
- The brain's an energy hog and needs a consistent diet of healthful food to function well.
- Drugs and alcohol harm short- and long-term memory.

"Learning" How to Be Addicted

Teens' predisposition to learn plays a critical role in the vexing issue of teenage drinking, smoking, and drug use. Neuroscientists have learned that addiction uses the same molecular pathways that are used in learning, most notably those involving the neurotransmitter dopamine. Repeated substance use permanently reshapes those pathways, researchers say. In fact, they now look at addiction as a form of learning: Adolescent rats are far more likely to become hooked than adults.

And epidemiological studies in humans suggest that the earlier someone starts using, the more likely he or she is to end up with big problems. Last month [in October 2008], a study tracking more than 1,000 people in New Zealand from age 3 to age 32 found that those who started drinking or using drugs regularly before age 15 were far more likely to fail in school, be convicted of a crime, or have substance abuse problems as an adult. "You can really screw up your brain at this point," says Jensen. "You're more vulnerable than you think." . . .

When Can the Brain Handle a Beer?

The new brain science has been used as a weapon by both sides of the drinking-age debate, though there is no definitive evidence for a "safe" age. "To say that 21 is based on the science of brain development is simply untrue," says John McCardell, president of Choose Responsibility, which advocates lowering the drinking age to 18. But there's also no scientific basis for choosing 18. The bottom line for now, most experts agree: Later is better.

Jay Giedd, an NIMH neuroscientist who pioneered the early MRI research on teen brains, is fond of saying that "what's important is the journey." Researchers caution that they can't prove links between brain parts and behavior, or that tackling adult-size challenges will turn teenagers into better adults. But common sense suggests that Nature had a reason to give adolescents strong bodies, impulsive natures, and curious, flexible minds. "Our generation is ready for more," insists Alex Harris, 20, of Gresham, Ore, who, with his twin brother, Brett, writes a blog and has published a book urging teens to push themselves. Its title: *Do Hard Things*.

SIX

Excessive Teen Texting and Social Networking May Signal Other Risky Behaviors

United Kingdom National Health Service

Researchers at Case Western Reserve School of Medicine in Cleveland, Ohio, used their own research and also data from the Youth Risk Behavior Survey to investigate whether there is a link between extreme social networking and health-related risky behavior in teens. The following viewpoint discusses their investigation and its results. The researchers concluded that there is a link between some risky behavior in teens (such as sexual activity, multiple sex partners, smoking, drinking, illegal drugs use, obesity, eating disorders, elevated stress levels, and suicidal thoughts) and hyper-texting (more than 120 texts a day) or hyper-networking (three hours or more per day on social-networking websites). No improved health habits were linked to excessive texting and networking. The results of this study were presented at the American Public Health Association's 138th Annual Meeting and Exposition and also reported in a press release from the United Kingdom National Health Service, which provides health care for all UK citizens.

NHS Choices, "Extreme Levels of Texting 'Unhealthy,'" November 10, 2010. www.nhs.uk.

"Feverish texting by your teenager may be a dangerous sign—they are more likely to have sex and binge drink," reported [London's] *Daily Telegraph*. The newspaper said research suggests that teenagers who "hyper-text", sending more than 120 texts a day, are more likely to have sex, drink and smoke.

This news report is based on a study presented at a US conference. More than 4,000 US teenagers were surveyed, and asked about their texting, social networking and other behaviours. Hyper-texting and hyper-networking (three or more hours a day of social networking) were found to be associated with various risky behaviours.

A recent study indicates that teens who hyper-text and hyper-network three or more hours a day are more likely to be involved in risky behaviors.

The study has not yet been published, making it difficult to appraise the reliability of its results. Despite the lack of detail, however, the cross-sectional nature of the survey means it cannot demonstrate cause and effect between different behaviours. The findings should not be applied to all teenagers in general. Hyper-texting is extreme behaviour, and it is not known how common it is in the UK.

This study shows that hyper-texting and -networking, as with most excessive behaviours, may indicate that other unhealthy behaviours co-exist.

Where Did the Story Come From?

The news reports are based on research publicised in a press release from the Case Western Reserve School of Medicine, Cleveland, Ohio in the US. The research has also been presented at the American Public Health Association's 138th Annual Meeting and Exposition. Full details of the study are not yet publicly available and this appraisal is reliant on the information in the press release and abstract.

The BBC [British Broadcasting Corporation], *Daily Telegraph* and *Daily Mail* covered this story, all of which based their articles mainly on the press release.

What Kind of Research Was This?

The researchers wanted to investigate whether the use of "communication technology", such as mobile phones and social networking, was associated with poor health behaviours among teens, including smoking, drinking and sexual activity. They were particularly interested in hyper-texting (120 or more texts a day) and hyper-networking (three or more hours a day on social networking sites).

The study design used was a cross-sectional survey, which investigates what is happening in a given population at a defined point in time. This type of study can only give an idea of how common behaviours or conditions are in that population, but cannot demonstrate cause and effect. As such, the study does not show that the level of texting has any causative association with the lifestyle behaviours examined, or any direct effect upon health.

There are likely to be many interacting personal, social and environmental factors that influence many of these behaviours and the findings of this localised cross-sectional survey should be generalised to the wider teenage population with caution.

What Were the Basic Findings?

The conference abstract and press release are brief and do not give details on how the study was carried out. The researchers are reported to have surveyed 4,257 high school students from an urban Midwestern county using the Youth Risk Behaviour Survey.

Hyper-texting was reported by 19.8% of students and hyper-networking by 11.5%. Almost a quarter of students reported no texting (22.5%) or online social networking (22.2%). Hyper-texting and networking were reported to occur more often among females, minority ethnic groups, and those of lower socioeconomic status.

Students who were classified as hyper-texters were three and half times more likely to have had sex. They had also had more sexual partners and 90% of those who hyper-texted reported having had four or more partners. Other health behaviours examined included smoking, with hyper-texters being 40% more likely to have tried cigarettes, alcohol use (two times more likely to have tried alcohol), binge drinking (43% more likely), and illegal drug use (41% more likely). Similar associations were observed with hyper-networking.

Hyper-texting and -networking students were also more likely to be obese or have an eating disorder, [or] miss school due to illness. They rated their own health as poorer and reported stress or suicidal thoughts. No better health outcomes were associated with texting and networking.

How Did the Researchers Interpret the Results?

The conclusion of the conference abstract is that "excessive use of communications technology among teens is related to higher levels of health risk behaviours and poorer health outcomes". In the press release, the lead researcher says:

"The startling results of this study suggest that when left unchecked, texting and other widely popular methods of staying connected can have dangerous health effects on teenagers.

"This should be a wake-up call for parents to not only help their children stay safe by not texting and driving, but by discouraging excessive use of the cellphone or social websites in general."

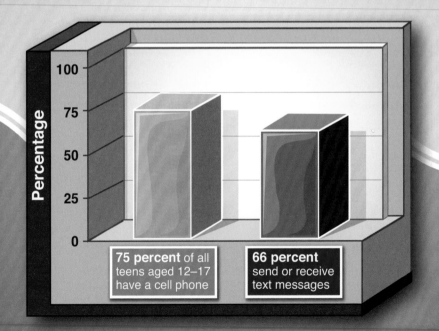

Cell Phone Use and Texting Among Teens

75 percent of all teens aged 12–17 have a cell phone

66 percent send or receive text messages

Conclusions Should Be Made Cautiously

These findings need to be interpreted with some caution. As yet, details of the study are not publicly available, making it difficult to appraise the methods used and how reliable the findings are.

As it stands, the survey results can only tell us of the prevalence of hyper-texting, hyper-networking and other health-related behaviours in this population of high school students in the US. One cannot apply cause and effect to these results, and this type of study cannot tell us whether or how these factors are related to each other. Also, this study was in the US, and behaviour in the UK may be different.

As such, the study provides no evidence that excessive texting causes other risky behaviours among teenagers. There is likely to be a complex interaction of many personal, social and environmental factors that influence many of these behaviours. Without further detail, it is not possible to determine how well the researchers took this into account, nor how well they explored the possible benefits of networking.

Hyper-texting is extreme behaviour, characterised by teenagers sending more than 120 texts a day. What this study highlights is that hyper-texting and -networking, as with most excessive behaviours, may indicate that other unhealthy behaviours co-exist.

SEVEN

Texting Can Teach Teens Positive Skills

Natalie Smith

Texting may be more beneficial than harmful for teens, according to Natalie Smith, associate editor for *Scholastic News*. Citing psychology and communication professors from major universities as well as teens who are avid texters, Smith explains that texting not only helps teens build and maintain supportive friendships, but it also helps them build communication skills. One professor found that texting has positive effects on the language and informal writing skills of teens. Another professor stated that texting helps teens develop the technical skills necessary for the digital world in which they live. Smith also overviews three dangers of texting and recommends that teens talk to their parents if they find themselves experiencing any of them.

Text messaging is Callie Owens's favorite way to communicate. The 17-year-old from Waynesboro, Virginia, sends 100 to 200 texts each day. She texts while she's hanging out with her friends, when she's working on her homework, and even during class!

Callie isn't alone. A recent survey by the Pew Internet and American Life Project found that one third of U.S. cell-phone users ages 12 to 17 send more than 100 texts daily. But not everyone is a fan of this constant stream of communication. "My parents tell me that I text too much," Callie tells *Choices*. "When I'm doing my homework, they'll ask, 'Isn't that distracting you?'"

Sound familiar? With texting on the rise, many parents worry that all the jabbering via keyboards is harmful to kids. But some experts say texting can actually benefit teens! "I think from everything we've seen, it's a good thing that they have more connections," says Larry Rosen, a psychology professor at California State University. Rosen studies how teens and families use and react to different types of technology.

Most parents think that perpetual texting is harmful. However, some experts say that, if it is used constructively, texting can improve teens' social, language, and technical skills.

Texting Benefits

Rosen admits constant texting can be unhealthy in some situations. But when texting is used constructively, experts say it can improve teens' social, language, and technical skills.

Texting—or sending short messages from one cell phone to another—first became available with major U.S. mobile-phone providers fewer than 10 years ago [from 2010]. Its popularity has grown rapidly, with teens texting more than any other age group. Texting is their primary medium for interacting with friends, according to the Pew survey.

"It's fast communication," says Jenny Kreps, 15, of Ridgefield, Connecticut. "I think it's easier than calling because you can still be doing something else while texting. You don't have to give your undivided attention to it."

But is all this texting turning teens into anti-social phone addicts? Scott Campbell, assistant professor of communication studies at the University of Michigan, has studied the role of cell phones in teens' lives and was a coauthor of the Pew survey. Campbell believes that texting is actually strengthening teens' social bonds.

Building Social Bonds

"They're using the technology to connect with their peers and be sociable, which is important for them at that point in life," Campbell says. "They're figuring out who they are and what they're about. The way they do that is through connections with other people."

Texting helps Matt Schlegel, 16, of Camp Hill, Pennsylvania, manage his social life. "I made a lot of friends when I was in my school musical," he says. "But I don't have classes with them because they're in different grades, so I'll text them to see how they're doing."

Some educators fear that texting encourages improper punctuation and sentence structure, which may negatively affect students' writing skills. Many researchers, though, disagree.

Rosen and his colleagues at California State University recently studied the relationship between "textisms" and formal and informal writing among young adults. Textisms are writing shortcuts such as LOL for "laughing out loud"; using emoticons (symbols that show facial expressions); or removing punctuation. The study found that texting could be having a positive influence on teens' language and communication skills. The young adults in the study who said they used more textisms demonstrated stronger informal writing abilities.

Tools to Talk

"I think anything done to communicate is good, and this is the most communicative generation in history because they've got the most tools to communicate with," Rosen says.

Other researchers agree. Campbell believes that sending and receiving texts allows teens to develop new technical skills. He says that this makes teens more competent communicators in the digital age. "It's just giving them their own language that they use," Campbell says. "It's a cultural thing. It has its own conventions. It has its own norms. It's like their own code teens can move in and out of a little."

Some teens say they have seen how texting can benefit communication skills. Jenny says text messaging has taught her to be more concise. "When writing out something, you can get directly to the point," she says. "Sometimes when you're talking, you get off topic. Texting gives you a chance to think of what you're saying before you actually say it."

Texting Troubles

Not everything about texting is great. Here are three problems:

1. *Texting into the night.* Some teens have trouble saying good night to their technology. According to the Pew survey, 84 percent of teens with cell phones sleep with their phone on or near their bed. Many teens say they text late into the night or wake up repeatedly to the buzz of an incoming text. Even a moderate amount of nighttime messaging can lead to long-term fatigue. Sleep deprivation can contribute to poor performance in school.

"But If You Don't Learn to Read and Write, How Are You Ever Going To Text?" Cartoon by David Carpenter/www.CartoonStock.com. © David Carpenter. Reproduction rights obtainable from www.CartoonStock.com.

2. *Texting while driving.* A recent survey by the Virginia Tech Transportation Institute found that when drivers text, they are 23 times more likely to crash their cars! And because they are less experienced behind the wheel than adults, teen drivers are even more likely to get into accidents. More than 20 states have passed laws making texting while driving illegal.

3. *Texting and doing nothing else.* "It's important to also not be connected once in a while," Campbell says. If you're skipping meals, homework, or other activities because of your

texting habits, it's time to scale back your texting. If you don't believe us, take the word of one of your peers: "People text me during church, and it drives me crazy," says Matt Schlegel. "I hate it. Get off your phone!"

If you think you're getting addicted to texting, talk to your parents about what to do. Together, make a plan to set texting limits. Come up with a specific maximum number of texts you can send each day. Speak to your friends about your change in texting habits. If you're nervous about them giving you a hard time, tell them your parents have changed your texting plan.

EIGHT

Sexting Is a Serious Issue

Joshua D. Herman

There is no question about it. Taking a nude or partially nude picture of anyone under the age of eighteen is a crime, even if that picture is of yourself, warns Joshua D. Herman, a lawyer who represents local governments and schools in Peoria, Illinois. In the following viewpoint Herman presents an overview of the child pornography laws that apply to "sexting,"—sending such photos over a cell phone—as well as discussing the laws' harsh consequences. Herman also gives advice to school districts on how to handle sexting if it is found on campus and how talking to teens and their parents about it before it happens is the best way to prevent it.

"Sexting" is a word you have probably heard but might not be able to define. For purposes of this article, "sexting" is the practice of sending nude or semi-nude pictures by cell phone or other electronic media; it is a sexual text ("sext") message. Sexting is a recent phenomenon, fueled by widespread availability of affordable mobile phones with picture-taking and sending capabilities.

It is increasingly common, especially among sexually curious, hormone-driven teenagers. On average, one in five teens has sent or posted nude or semi-nude pictures or videos of themselves. Although just over two-thirds of those teens meant those images for their boyfriend or girlfriend, 25 percent of teen girls and 33 percent of teen boys admit they have had sext messages meant for someone else shared with them.

Among teens, sexting is ordinary and somewhat accepted, even though a majority of teens know sexting "can have serious negative consequences." Most, however, do not know it is a crime.

Adults risk embarrassment if their sext message is misdirected. But when a teenager (meaning a minor between 13 and 17) creates, sends, or receives a sext message in Illinois, he or she may have committed the criminal offense of child pornography. Sex offense

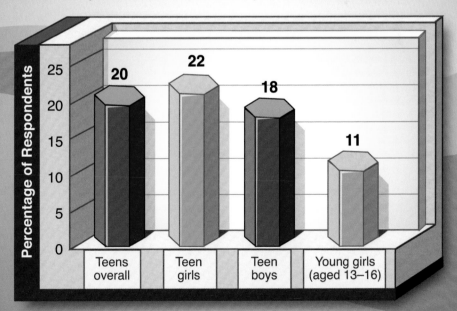

Teens and Sexting

What percentage of teens say they have sent or posted nude or seminude pictures of themselves?

Taken from: The National Campaign to Prevent Teen Pregnancy, "Sex and Tech: Results from a Survey of Teens and Young Adults," September 25–October 3, 2008. www.thenationalcampaign.org/sextech_Summary.PDF.

laws predating the sexting phenomenon do not contemplate the ease and frequency with which teens send risqué pictures to each other from their phones. Nonetheless, they subject sexting teens to a myriad of felony charges and branding as a "sex offender."

A teenager's ability to snap a picture and send it in seconds without reflection gives rise to new legal issues for society and the legal community. Teen sexting confronts attorneys and courts with new and complicated legal issues. Across the nation, prosecutors and police are not yet uniform in applying these laws to the minors they were meant to protect. Criminal and juvenile courts must also ponder applying severe criminal penalties to youth who may have merely had a moment of poor judgment.

Moreover, a sexting teen's social and legal problems often converge at the schoolhouse door. For attorneys who counsel educational institutions, it is only a matter of time before they must grapple with sexting-related issues.

These issues pose difficult challenges for school administrators and staff, especially where improper investigation can subject school personnel to prosecution for the same criminal offenses that teens risk by sexting. By being aware of the relevant law and having policies in place to deal with sexting, prosecutors and law enforcement, school districts, parents, and teenagers themselves can curb sexting behavior while avoiding liability.

The Crime of Sexting

Sexting can have serious social and emotional consequences for teens and adults alike—especially where a picture is taken without knowledge, forwarded without consent, or used to bully and harass. Further, the embarrassment of uncontrolled dissemination of personal and private pictures can significantly disrupt the teen's life.

For example, after hundreds of people were sent sext messages a teen had sent only to her boyfriend, she was cruelly harassed through MySpace and Facebook, leading her to hang herself. In addition to risking reputation and self-esteem, sexting teenagers also expose themselves, their peers, and their school administrators to significant criminal liability.

Child Pornography

Most alarmingly, a sexting minor, or a recipient of a sext message from a minor, may have committed one or more felonies under the Illinois Child Pornography Act (the "Act"). Offenses under the Act are generally Class 1 felonies, punishable by fines ranging from $1,000 to $100,000 and imprisonment for four to 15 years.

In Illinois, a person commits the offense of child pornography by *videotaping or photographing* anyone he or she should know is under the age of 18 and who is engaged in any sexual act or in any pose involving lewd exhibition of unclothed or transparently clothed genitals, pubic area, buttocks, or female breast. *There is no exception for taking pictures of oneself.* Thus, a 17-year-old who snaps his or her own revealing picture has technically created child pornography, a Class 1 felony with a mandatory fine of between $2,000 and $100,000 and at least four years in prison. It would not be a crime if the teen were 18.

Soliciting or enticing someone one should know is under the age of 18 to appear in such a picture or videotape is also a child pornography offense. Thus, a 16-year-old boy violates the Act if he asks his 16-year-old girlfriend to send him a semi-naked picture. If the youth is 17 or older and uses the Internet to solicit the sext message from a minor, he or she may also be charged with "indecent solicitation of a child," a Class 4 felony.

Forwarding a sext message to others may also constitute the offense of child pornography. *Reproducing or disseminating* such pictures of a person one should know is under the age of 18 is an offense of child pornography. A teen who sends his or her *own picture* to another also violates this provision.

A person who, knowing its content or nature, *possesses* a photograph or film depicting someone he or she should know is under 18 has also violated the Act. If the possession is involuntary, the possessor has a defense. Possession is voluntary where a person "knowingly procures or receives" the illicit material "with sufficient time to terminate his or her possession of it."

While the statute does not define "sufficient time," sooner is better than later. Finding and deleting an unsolicited sext message an hour after its receipt better demonstrates involuntary possession than does carrying a sext message on the phone for two months or more.

The Act dictates that cell phones used for sexting by minors must be *seized and forfeited*, allowing "law enforcement or prosecuting officers" to possess offending materials as part of the "performance of [their] official duties." School administrators get no such protection when investigating incidents of sexting among students. Consequently, school officials must investigate sexting cautiously because, like teens, they may also be charged with possessing child pornography.

Further, minors who sext across state lines (by using the Internet, for example), or by using materials that traveled in interstate commerce, are also subject to federal charges of child pornography. For example, students who post prohibited pictures on their Facebook pages have likely violated federal criminal law.

Sex Offender Registry

In Illinois, someone who commits the offense of child pornography is a "sex offender" and must register and report as such. Not only is non-compliance with reporting a felony, but even compliant individuals face the shame and scrutiny of public reporting.

Beyond registering and reporting as sex offenders, students convicted of child pornography may also be bound by other restrictions that can significantly complicate their lives. For example, child sex offenders 17 and older cannot be present on school grounds or loiter or reside within 500 feet of the school building. Revealing that these laws do not contemplate school children, there are exceptions for sex offenders who are *parents* of students, allowing them to be on school grounds in particular circumstances, but no such exception exists for *student* sex offenders.

The following example places the foregoing offenses in perspective: a 16-year-old girl who snaps a sexual, semi-nude picture of herself to send as a phone message to her boyfriend has committed at least three felonies by creating, disseminating, and possessing "child pornography." If her boyfriend requested she send the sext message, he is subject to at least two felonies: soliciting and voluntarily possessing the sext message. Thus, one unwise youthful indiscretion results in five felonies and subjects the teenage couple to branding as "sex offenders."

Although some states consider sexting by teens to be a criminal offense, other states are attempting to decriminalize the practice in cases where minors are involved.

A Legislative Response

Some states have attempted to decriminalize sexting among teens, or at least reduce the offense from felony to misdemeanor. For example, Vermont recently enacted a law making a teenager's first "sexting" offense a juvenile court matter, giving the teen the opportunity to be sent to a diversionary program rather than be charged as an adult and branded a sex offender.

As this article went to press [in April 2010], the Illinois Senate had just passed SB 2513, which would transform most sexting between teens from a felony to a noncrime by treating the teen in question as a nondelinquent minor in need of supervision under the Juvenile Court Act. Enacting this bill or one like it into law would be a huge step in the right direction.

Solving Sexting?

Cell phones have become ubiquitous among students, but the law has been slow to catch up. Illinois legislators should continue to examine incidents of sexting and how the current law applies to them. Legislators should consider drafting a narrow exception to sex offenses to prevent "innocent" teens from being charged with serious violations while maintaining liability for those who are guilty of actual child pornography—regardless of age.

Until then, parents and schools may be better equipped to discipline and admonish sexting teens than are police and prosecutors. Because of their age, a vast majority of sexting teenagers attend school. Thus, even if the likelihood that sexting teens will be charged with a felony is remote, school districts cannot ignore the disruptive and potentially tragic consequences of sexting among their students.

School districts should work with local law enforcement in establishing district policies and procedures for investigating allegations of sexting. They should discuss whether and how, if at all, law enforcement will be involved in sexting issues. Because determining what constitutes criminal "child pornography" can be difficult even for those in law enforcement, Dave Haslett, Chief of the Illinois Attorney General's High Tech Crimes Bureau, suggests that schools involve law enforcement early to avoid missteps.

Based on this dialogue with law enforcement, the school district should revise its policy and procedure accordingly. Additionally, school districts should educate their students about the pitfalls and criminal consequences of sexting.

No Cell Phones

Naturally, prohibiting student use of cell phones during the school day can greatly reduce sexting issues at school. Because students may still use computers to send, request, or view offending material, school districts should also consider a broader policy prohibiting the creation, possession, or dissemination of obscene or profane materials by students, regardless of the device(s) used.

Confirm Violation of School Policy

A school should confirm whether a student alleged to have sexted actually violated school policy. Establishing improper conduct will be easier where the district has explicitly defined inappropriate behavior with regard to sexting in its prohibited conduct policy.

Take the Cell Phone

According to attorney Daniel Spillman of the Illinois Attorney General's High Tech Crimes Bureau, possession of a sext message that is child pornography is no different than possessing a "kilo of cocaine." He advises school administrators to immediately confiscate devices with such material on them and report the incident to law enforcement immediately.

Beyond reducing school district exposure, confiscating the device containing the sext message will prevent further dissemination, further harm to any victims, and allow for an investigation of other students that may have been involved or harmed. Involving law enforcement early will also minimize any potential criminal liability of school personnel.

Report Incident to Victim

The student pictured in a sext message may be unaware of his or her victimization. Schools should consider when and how they should inform such a student, giving thought to the sensitive nature of the subject and the student's right to privacy. Schools may also consider coordinating this task with local law enforcement and guidance counselors.

Discipline the Student(s)

Administrators should establish a uniform method for disciplining students involved in sexting. When disciplining sexting students, school personnel should consider the facts of the situation and review district policies related to sexual harassment, bullying, indecent or profane materials, use of electronic devices, and failures to abide by student handbook guidelines.

Educate Teens and Their Families

The school district should educate students and parents about sexting and school policies related to the behavior. Many teens, even if they do not sext, consider it "normal" and do not understand sexting is a crime. Many parents are unaware of the phenomenon's pervasiveness or its consequences.

Families should discuss the legal and moral issues surrounding sexting. Parents should frequently review their child's social media, e.g., messages on cell phones, Facebook, MySpace, etc., and set rules for the use of such media. Teenagers and their families should also review their school's policies related to electronic devices and prohibited student conduct.

Teens should not create, possess, solicit, or send/forward sext messages. Teens possessing such messages *involuntarily* have a defense. To ensure the efficacy of this defense, teens must be vigilant in discovering and deleting sext messages.

Lawyers counseling a minor accused of sexting and violating child pornography laws should also consider the minor's role in the creation, dissemination, or possession of the offending material to appreciate potential exposure to other criminal charges. Lawyers should also explore whether a teen's actions give rise to civil liability for claims such as invasion of privacy or defamation.

Finally, although child pornography laws generally regard minors as the victim, prosecuting sexting teens for a strict-liability child pornography offense may be punishing them for their age rather than the content of a sext. Thus, lawyers should also consider whether the content of a sext message constitutes child pornography or is protected speech under the First Amendment.

What Next?

On average, one in every five teens at a school near you is sexting. Until the Illinois General Assembly [state legislature] amends the criminal code to account for the unforeseen teenage use of technology in violation of the law, sexting will continue to be an increasing social and legal problem. Thus, prosecutors and attorneys for these sexting teens, their parents, and their school districts should be prepared to educate and advise their clients about the social and legal ramifications of sexting.

NINE

The Courts Should Not Overreact to Teen Sexting

Art Bowker and Michael Sullivan

While sexting involving minors is illegal and can ruin lives, some teens who take and send nude pictures of themselves or others are being punished too harshly and are inappropriately labeled as sex offenders, according to this viewpoint by Art Bowker, a cybercrime specialist, and Michael Sullivan, an assistant US attorney. Bowker and Sullivan urge law enforcement officers to carefully consider the details of each sexting case and charge minors appropriately. They also discuss some measures that lawmakers are taking in some states to make the laws more appropriate, but they also recognize how difficult it will be for lawmakers to do that while still protecting minors.

Juvenile sexting is increasing in frequency. A recent study found that 20 percent of teenagers (22 percent of girls and 18 percent of boys) sent naked or seminude images of themselves or posted them online. Another survey indicated that nearly 1 of 6 teens between the ages of 12 and 17 who own cell phones have received naked or nearly nude pictures via text message from someone they know.

Many disturbing examples of such behavior exist. For instance, two 15 year olds, a male and a female, were sentenced in juvenile

Art Bowker and Michael Sullivan, "Sexting: Risky Actions and Overreactions," *FBI Law Enforcement Bulletin*, July 2010, vol. 79, issue 7, pp. 27–31. Copyright © 2010 by the FBI. All rights reserved. Reproduced with permission.

court for possessing and sending nude photos on their cell phones; the girl sent a picture of herself to the boy, and another image allegedly was taken on his camera. A 15-year-old boy received 12 months of probation for forwarding a picture of his private parts to a 13-year-old girl's cell phone. An 18-year-old high school graduate committed suicide after a nude photo she had transmitted via her cell phone to her boyfriend also was sent to hundreds of teenagers in her school. Other students, who apparently continued to forward the image, allegedly harassed the girl. Law enforcement officers and prosecutors face increased pressure to handle these cases as effectively as possible.

Sexting Can Have Tragic Consequences

Sexting can result in tragic circumstances, such as the previously noted suicide. Additionally troubling, adults may participate in the activity. However, aggressive prosecution of all juvenile sexting cases also can present problems. In one instance, a local prosecutor was named as a federal defendant in a civil lawsuit after he attempted to take corrective action over images he considered questionable. Through their parents, the involved juveniles brought the suit to prevent their prosecution after they refused to complete the prosecutor's suggested diversion/education program. The U.S. District Court in Pennsylvania granted a temporary restraining order to prevent the prosecutor from bringing criminal charges against the juvenile plaintiffs over the images. Also problematic, the social implications for an inappropriate sex offender registration label resulting from juvenile adjudication require careful consideration. The registration requirements can apply to young people and, depending upon the circumstances, can extend well into adulthood. Investigators, with prosecutorial direction, can develop appropriate guidelines to chart a legal course to avoid extreme actions.

Misconduct

To determine the appropriate response, law enforcement officers must carefully consider the alleged misconduct and determine if it falls into one of two categories. First, is the image or communication illegal? For instance, the definition found in the federal child pornography statute, 18 U.S.C. § 2256, refers to illegal images with minors as those involving sexually explicit conduct. Does the picture meet this definition or one in a particular state statute? Additionally, investigators should consider whether the communication might be harassing or menacing to the party in the image or the recipient of it.

Second, did any illegal use of a computer occur in the communication? For instance, a youth involved in viewing, transmitting, or storing inappropriate pictures on school equipment might face legal difficulty for unauthorized use or damages. The cleanup and removal of these images can be costly for schools.

Obviously, these categories can overlap. However, this can shed light on alternative charges that may not be as apparent if someone views the misconduct solely as a sex offense. For example, a 15-year-old male posts an inappropriate image of himself on the school computer as a prank. Charging the youth as a sex offender may be a gross overstatement, possibly resulting in a sex-offender-registration issue. Perhaps, charging him as a delinquent for damaging school property due to the cost of removing the offensive image may be a more appropriate response.

Offenders

While an adult's active involvement in juvenile sexting always should result in the strong consideration of charges, cases involving only youths may call for a different, more fluid approach. To this end, investigators should analyze the subject of the images, the victim. How old is the victim? Did she know about the photograph? Did the victim take it herself without the encouragement or direct participation of any other person? Did she forward the picture to anyone? What is the age difference between the victim and the recipient of the image? Does she now face harassment because of her inappropriate behavior? Who is harassing her, and are charges warranted against them? The answers to these questions can help indicate if the subject of the image is a true victim in every sense of the word.

Although, perhaps, not in the image, the youth offender somehow took part in the juvenile sexting. His actions could include soliciting the picture or actively participating in creating, possessing, receiving, or distributing the image. Did he request the picture, or did someone just send it to him? Did he keep it or forward it on? Why? To embarrass or harass the victim? What is or was the relationship between the youth offender and victim? How old are they, and what is the age difference between them?

It may be a mitigating factor where there is little or no disparity in age. However, if the offender is significantly older (e.g., a 15-year-old with pictures of an 8-year-old), authorities have serious misconduct issues to address. Has the perpetrator participated in

Parents attend a seminar on sexting sponsored by the Connecticut State Police. Authorities have chosen not to prosecute many incidents of sexting, instead asking parents to discipline their children.

similar misconduct in the past? Consideration of these factors can help investigators and prosecutors decide the proper course of action, such as no charges, diversion, or formal charges (sex or nonsex offense).

Prevention

As the first line of defense against this problem, law enforcement personnel and educators should provide regular presentations—and numerous excellent information sources exist to draw from—to young people on Internet safety and the repercussions of inappropriate online behavior. Digital images do not deteriorate over time and easily can spread worldwide. Youths need to understand that what they do online may have a very long existence. Such presentations can help minimize or prevent future occurrences of juvenile sexting. They also can be used as a component in developing diversion programs.

Additional Investigative Areas

In cases where the images clearly involve child pornography, law enforcement needs to contact the National Center for Missing and Exploited Children (NCMEC), which operates the Child Victim Identification Program, the national clearinghouse for child pornography cases and the main point of contact for international agencies concerning child pornography victims. By forwarding information regarding known victims, prosecutors can obtain convictions of other perpetrators who may possess these images long after the juvenile sexting case has been initially investigated.

Legislative Remedies

In 2009, state law makers, most notably in Ohio, Utah, and Vermont, began considering legislative solutions. One early proposal was a blanket decriminalization of juvenile sexting. Such a questionable approach has the real potential of putting youths at risk by inadvertently excluding sexting offenses committed by

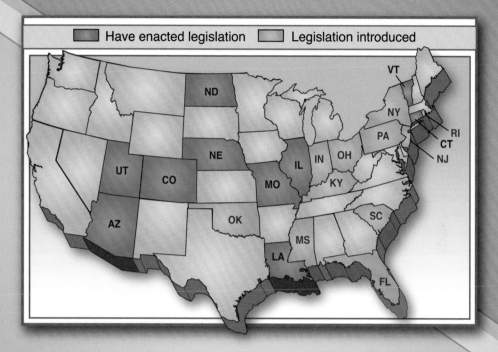

Have enacted legislation   Legislation introduced

Taken from: Nathan Koppel and Ashby Jones, "Are 'Sext' Messages a Teenage Felony or Folly?," *Wall Street Journal*, August 25, 2010. Sources: National Conference of State Legislatures; Berkman Center for Internet & Society at Harvard University.

older juveniles against younger ones. Recently, Vermont stepped back from this extreme, opting to reclassify juvenile sexting cases from felony to misdemeanor offenses as long as the acts were consensual. The debate, no doubt, will continue, but legislatures must be careful to not enact laws that put youths at risk.

The Challenge

Juvenile sexting poses a challenge for numerous groups to act responsibly with common sense and sound discretion. Law enforcement officers and prosecutors must keep in mind that juvenile sex and child pornography laws exist to protect young people. While the activity associated with juvenile sexting technically may violate criminal statutes, prosecutors must use discretion, vested with their position, to confront the activity appropriately. Every act violating a statute should not necessarily bring charges. Legislators must avoid the urge to legislate away instances of an abuse of prosecutorial discretion. A well-intentioned law designed to undo a perceived overreaction by one prosecutor may unintentionally prevent the prosecution of a youth exploiting a much younger child.

Parents must remain involved in their children's lives and not surrender their parental oversight to a fear of technology. And, young people need to learn to use technology responsibly. Everyone has a role in protecting youths, and they need to fulfill that responsibility with common sense and sound discretion.

TEN

Legislation Can Curb Teens' Texting While Driving

Matt Sundeen

> Whether it is trying the latest stunt, not wearing a seat-belt, or just driving too fast, teens often take risks behind the wheel. Risky teen driving behavior having to do with distractions—especially cell phones and texting—is the focus of this viewpoint, however. In it, Matt Sundeen, a transportation expert at the National Conference of State Legislatures, discusses many of these distractions as well as some of the measures state lawmakers are taking in an attempt to prevent them.

On a June night in 2007, a fiery head-on collision killed five young women in upstate New York. The victims, all of whom had graduated from high school five days earlier, died instantly when their sports utility vehicle swerved cross a two-lane road into oncoming traffic and slammed into a tractor trailer. According to the police, a flurry of text messages and phone calls were sent on the 17-year-old driver's cell phone moments before the accident. This distraction, the driver's inexperience behind the wheel, the vehicle's high rate of speed and the time of day were all cited as likely factors in the crash.

Unfortunately, the tragedy in New York vividly demonstrated something that parents and traffic safety experts have known for

Matt Sundeen, "Driving While Distracted: Inexperienced Teen Drivers Too Often Take Fatal Risks," *State Legislatures*, vol. 34, no. 5, May 2008. Copyright © by The National Conference of State Legislatures. All rights reserved. Reproduced by permission.

years: Teens generally don't make good drivers. Inexperienced teen drivers are more easily distracted than others. Behind the wheel they are less likely to recognize and react quickly to dangerous driving conditions. New drivers, particularly young men, often show off and are prone to taking risks.

Although teens drive less than all but the oldest drivers, they account for a disproportionate number of fatal accidents. The crash rate per mile driven for 16- to 19-year-olds is four times higher than the rate for older drivers, and motor vehicle crashes are the leading cause of death among 13- to 19-year-olds in the United States.

Teen Licensing Laws

For years, state lawmakers have attempted to improve teen driver safety through changes in licensing requirements, known as graduated driver licensing. These state laws most often include limits on nighttime driving and restrictions on the number of unrelated passengers allowed in the car. Although most traffic safety experts still believe these laws provide the best chance to improve safety, state lawmakers are now addressing a new phenomenon that perhaps affects teens more acutely than any other demographic: driver distraction.

"The combination of inexperience and distraction is highly dangerous in younger drivers," says Arizona Representative Steve Farley, who is sponsoring several bills this year [2008] that he hopes will curb teen driver distraction. "Distracted driving can be as impairing as drunk driving. It's been a big problem here and I knew that I had do something about it."

Experts estimate that as many as 80 percent of motor vehicle crashes and 65 percent of near crashes have driver inattention as a contributing cause. Each year in the United States, the 4.9 million driver distraction related crashes kill approximately 34,400 people, cause 2.1 million injuries and trigger as much as $184 billion in property damage.

A virtually limitless list of events and activities, both inside and outside the vehicle, have the potential to distract. In a 2007

Lawmakers in every state have considered some sort of restrictions on cell phone use while driving, and more than half of the states have passed laws to regulate the behavior.

Nationwide Insurance survey, drivers confessed to a laundry list of misbehaviors while driving that included daydreaming, fixing their hair, texting, comforting children and putting pets in their lap. They also acknowledged switching seats with passengers, reading books, writing grocery lists, watching movies, nursing babies, putting in contacts, painting toenails, urinating out the car window, shaving and changing shoes.

The Safety of Cell Phones

The most common distracting activity is using a cell phone or other wireless device such as a BlackBerry. CTIA, the international association of the wireless telecommunications industry, reports that wireless communications devices are found in 81 percent of households, and more than 255 million people now subscribe to wireless services in the United States. Experts estimate that as many 73 percent of drivers use their cell phone.

Clearly, these figures have grabbed the attention of legislators. Within the last five years [2004–2008], lawmakers in every state have considered some sort of restriction on cell phones in the car, and 29 states and the District of Columbia have passed laws to regulate cell phone use while driving. The strictest provisions, found in six states, the District of Columbia, and many local communities, prohibit all drivers from using hand-held wireless communication devices.

Enforcement of these laws can be difficult, but since 2001, when New York passed its total ban on using hand-held devices, a million people have been ticketed.

Targeting the Young

The new trend in states, however, is to specifically target younger drivers. Studies have found that drivers between the ages of 16 and 24 are twice as likely than older drivers to use the phone. In 2003, the National Transportation Safety Board recommended that states limit or completely prohibit young drivers from using cell phones. Since then, 17 states have passed such restrictions.

California and Maine prohibit all teenage drivers from using any wireless communications device while operating a motor vehicle. Fifteen other states and the District of Columbia prohibit drivers who have only a learner's permit from using them. As of March [2008], legislatures in 16 other states were considering similar restrictions.

"I introduced the bill because I thought it would save lives," says Senator Joe Simitian, who sponsored California's law. "The

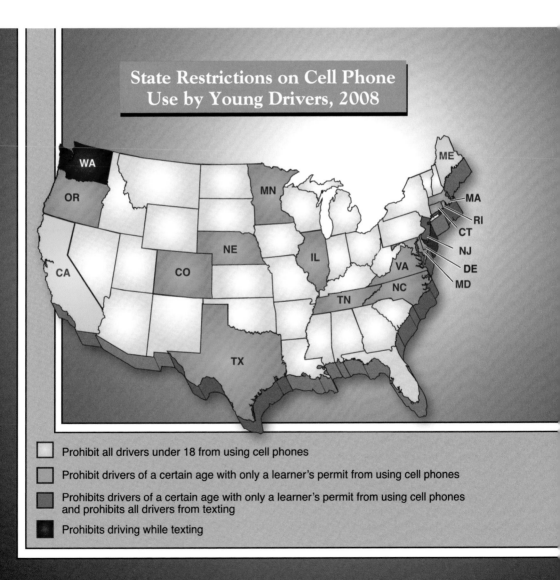

State Restrictions on Cell Phone Use by Young Drivers, 2008

☐ Prohibit all drivers under 18 from using cell phones

☐ Prohibit drivers of a certain age with only a learner's permit from using cell phones

☐ Prohibits drivers of a certain age with only a learner's permit from using cell phones and prohibits all drivers from texting

■ Prohibits driving while texting

data about teenage driver safety are really compelling, and I had no opposition to the restriction. Parents come up to me all the time and thank me for the bill. In a lot of ways the public is ahead of the Legislature on this issue."

Texting Troubles, Too

Legislators are also addressing a relatively new cell phone danger, known as driving while texting, that seems to disproportionately affect younger motorists. It's estimated that wireless subscribers send approximately 158 billion text messages in the United States each year. Although the exact number of text messages sent or received by people who are driving is unknown, a recent survey found that 20 percent of drivers admit to doing it. The rate, however, is much higher for younger drivers. The same survey found that a whopping 66 percent of drivers ages 18 through 24 use wireless devices to send or receive text messages while driving.

"I visited a high school class two years ago and was shocked at how many kids told me they text while driving," says Washington Representative Joyce McDonald. "It's obvious that it's a lethal combination. I read that average drivers take their eyes off the road something like 14 times every 30 seconds if they are texting. When you are driving fast on the highway, it's not a place to take more risks."

A 2007 Harris Interactive poll found that 91 percent of Americans think that driving while texting is as dangerous as drunk driving, and 89 percent of Americans support prohibitions on driving while texting. State legislators are taking notice. In 2007, Washington legislators passed the first law to specifically prohibit sending or receiving text messages while driving. New Jersey passed a similar restriction soon after, but, differing from Washington, chose to enforce its law as a primary offense. At least 21 states were considering such proposals as of March [2008].

It seems likely that as texting and cell phone use factor more often in crashes such as the one in New York, more states will look at restrictions on younger drivers.

"You can't take other people's lives into your hands with this kind of behavior," says Washington's McDonald. "I just hope this law helps."

ELEVEN

Teens Ignore Laws to Curb Texting While Driving

Dan Whitcomb

> With estimates that 1 trillion text messages were sent in the United States in 2009 alone—and the fact that drivers who text are twenty-three times more likely to be involved in an accident—texting while driving is nothing to ignore. In this selection Dan Whitcomb, a Los Angeles reporter for Reuters news service, explains that teens are likely to ignore laws that prohibit cell phone use while driving. Whitcomb cites statistics from law enforcement showing that a ban on texting while driving is difficult to enforce. As a result, says Whitcomb—in states where both texting and phoning while driving are illegal—both law officers and teens report that one is far less likely to be ticketed for texting. It is simply easier for officers to see someone talking on a phone than texting.

Karen Cordova, a 17-year-old high school student and part-time supermarket cashier, admits she sometimes texts friends while driving home from work late at night, lonely and bored.

The Arizona teenager knows it's illegal in Phoenix and dangerous. She once almost drifted into oncoming traffic while looking at her phone.

But would a nationwide ban stop Cordova and her friends from texting in their cars? No way, she said.

"Nobody is going to listen," Cordova said.

With momentum building in Washington for all 50 U.S. states to outlaw text messaging behind the wheel, there is evidence that the key demographic targeted by such legislation, teen drivers, will not pay much attention.

At least one major study has found that, with mobile devices now central to their lives, young people often ignore laws against using cell phones or texting in the car.

The number of text messages is up tenfold in the past three years and Americans sent an estimated 1 trillion in 2009.

Fewer Tickets for Texting

Some police agencies, while strongly in favor of such mandates, say it's tough for officers to enforce them.

The California Highway Patrol [CHP] has handed out nearly 163,000 tickets to drivers talking on handheld phones since mid-2008. But it has issued only 1,400 texting citations since January in a state of 23 million drivers—not for lack of trying.

"The handheld cell phone is relatively easy for us to spot, we can see when somebody has their phone up to their ear," CHP spokeswoman Fran Clader said.

"But with the texting it's a little bit more of a challenge to catch them in the act, because we have to see it and if they are holding it down in their lap it's going to be harder for us to see."

Already 19 states and the District of Columbia ban texting by all drivers, while 9 others prohibit it by young drivers.

Texting Causes Accidents

In July [2009], Democratic Senator Chuck Schumer, citing a study that found texting drivers were 23 times more likely to be in an accident, introduced a bill requiring states to prohibit the practice or risk losing federal highway funds.

Since then, Senator Jay Rockefeller has offered his own bill that would achieve the ban through grants to states.

Teens and Distracted Driving

Have you ever experienced or done any of the following?

Distraction	All teens 12–17	Older teens 12–17	Cell users aged 16–17	Texters aged 16–17
Been in a car when the driver was texting	48	64	70	73
Been in a car when the driver used a cell phone in a way that put themselves or others in danger	40	48	51	52
Talked on a cell phone while driving	n/a	43	52	54
Texted while driving	n/a	26	32	34

Percentage

In October [2009], during a three-day conference in Washington on distracted driving, President Barack Obama signed an executive order barring federal employees from texting behind the wheel.

Transportation Secretary Ray LaHood said he would seek to expand that rule to bus drivers and truckers who cross state lines and called the conference "probably the most important meeting in the history of the Department of Transportation."

But a much-cited study by the Insurance Institute for Highway Safety found that usage of cell phones for calls and texting in North Carolina actually ticked up slightly after the state banned them for drivers under the age of 18.

A study by the Automobile Club of Southern California found that texting by drivers dropped after the state's law took effect, but it did not break down the data by age.

"What I would say is that texting and cell phone devices have become such a component of life for teens and for young people that it's hard for them to differentiate between doing something normal and doing something wrong," said Steven Bloch, senior research associate for the Automobile Club.

The problem is not unique to the United States. In Britain, a public service announcement on texting while driving drew worldwide attention for its extremely graphic imagery.

The spot shows three texting teen girls in a horrific head-on collision with another car, and lingers on shots of their bloodied

Studies have shown that teens who text while driving are twenty-three times more likely to have an accident than those who do not.

faces shattering the windshield as a child whose parents have been killed cries for her dead mother to wake up.

Phoenix Bans Texting

In 2007, Phoenix became one of the first U.S. cities to ban texting while driving, although Arizona still has no statewide law.

Out of a group of four high school students interviewed by Reuters in Phoenix, three admitted texting while driving and a fourth said he had stopped only after his cousin caused a serious traffic accident while sending a message.

Cordova's classmate, 17-year-old Anna Hauer, says she often texts her boyfriend when she drives and doubts she or her friends would stop because of new legislation.

"By the time they pull you over, the chances are you are going to be done with your text anyway so they can't exactly prove that you were texting," she said.

TWELVE

Risky Teen Driving Behavior Can Be Deadly

Jeremy Roebuck

Teens have been taking risks with cars since the automobile was invented and movies have been glamorizing risky driving probably for as long. That does not make the deadly consequences of risky driving stunts less real, however, as one Pennsylvania teen discovered. In the following viewpoint *Philadelphia Inquirer* staff writer Jeremy Roebuck describes the sentencing of this teen and the risky maneuver that the teen was attempting when his car struck an elderly pedestrian who died from injuries three days later. Just one day before the accident, a friend of the teen had warned him that someone was likely to get hurt if he continued his risky behavior.

Fingers clenched before him, Colin Murphy haltingly described the anguish he said he had felt since killing an elderly pedestrian earlier this year during an attempt at a daredevil driving maneuver known as "drifting."

"I think about it every day," the 17-year-old said, his speech punctuated by sobs, as he addressed juvenile court in Montgomery County [Pennsylvania]. "Driving reckless can change your life at any moment. I wish young drivers would realize that."

The aftermath of that October day's events—pulling his emergency brake at top speeds, losing control of his car, and striking 81-year-old Zita Egitto as she walked down a residential street in Upper Moreland Township—has been tough for the Willow Grove boy to process. On Monday [December 13, 2010], he began a multi-month sentence at a residential youth treatment facility after pleading guilty to charges of homicide by a vehicle.

But for enthusiasts of the risky drifting technique, Murphy's case is the latest in a long string of setbacks for a sport still seeking legitimacy in the racing world.

"It gives what we do a bad name," said Matt Petty, a promoter at a Monmouth County, N.J.–based series of drifting events called Club Loose. "It kind of opens your eyes to the fact that we're not doing a great job educating kids."

Hollywood movies, such as The Fast and the Furious: Tokyo Drift, *have glamorized car drifting, motivating teens to try it.*

After first emerging as a popular racing maneuver in Japan, drifting has slowly developed into a competitive motor sport in its own right during the last 15 years. Achieved by pulling on the emergency brake while driving at top speeds and sharply turning the steering wheel, the maneuver is capable of sending cars into a sideways slide.

But until the release of the 2006 action movie *The Fast and the Furious: Tokyo Drift*, most outside the racing world were unfamiliar with the precarious practice and most inside gave it little respect.

The film—and its depictions of drivers skidding through parking garages and along Tokyo's busy streets—sent a whole new audience out of movie theater parking lots and onto public roads with tires screeching in their wake, Petty said.

"The movie brought a lot of money into our sport and upped the overall legitimacy," he said. "But at the same time, it inspired a lot of kids who didn't know what they were doing."

Montgomery County Juvenile Court Judge Wendy Demchick-Alloy took pains to emphasize the consequences of that ignorance at Murphy's sentencing hearing Monday. Demchick-Alloy ordered the teen to pay more than $10,000 in restitution along with serving a term at the George Junior Republic facility outside Pittsburgh, where he must complete a program that can take anywhere from months to years.

"This is not a movie," she chided the teen from the bench. "This is not *Fast and Furious*. This is not *Tokyo Drift*. You were behind the wheel of a dangerous weapon."

Murphy exhibited little awareness of that danger in the weeks before striking Egitto, witnesses testified Monday. He practiced drifting in busy parking lots during peak business hours. At one point, a friend riding with him warned that by "doing things like this, someone's going to get hurt," said Detective Robert Kerrigan of the Upper Moreland Township Police Department.

On Oct. 12, one day after that warning, Murphy's next drifting attempt ended in death.

Yanking back the emergency brake of his Volkswagen Passat while speeding along Old York Road, Murphy collided with

Egitto, who was walking on the sidewalk to the home of a 95-year-old friend. The car whipped into her with such force that she was catapulted onto the porch of a nearby home.

She died of her injuries three days later.

"This was beyond devastating for all of us," said Frank Egitto, one of Zita Egitto's five adult sons. "The loss we feel is beyond words."

Incidents by untrained drivers and on public roads have led to fatal wrecks across the country, including a 2007 incident that killed four teens in Bristol, Conn.

Percent Distribution of All Deaths to US Teenagers 12–19 Years, by Cause of Death, 1999–2006

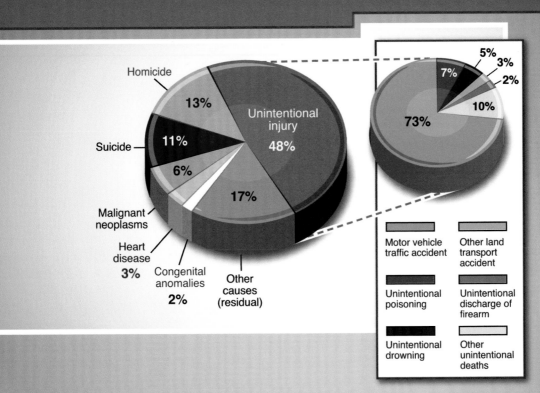

Taken from: Centers for Disease Control and Prevention/National Center for Health Statistics, "Percent Distribution of All Deaths to Teenagers 12–19 Years, by Cause of Death: 1999–2006," NCHS Data Brief no. 37, May 2010. www.cdc.gov/nchs/data/databriefs/db37.htm.

Petty, the New Jersey drifting promoter, recalls his own early days drifting his car into ditches and embankments along roads trafficked by other drivers. He now hosts regular meet-ups for drifters at the Old Bridge Township Raceway Park in Englishtown, N.J.—an alternative that allows drivers to practice in a controlled environment without endangering other motorists.

"It was stupid for us. We were naive," he said. "We didn't know any better."

For Murphy, that realization came too late.

"I never meant for anyone to be hurt," he said, shortly before being led from the courtroom. "I just wish this never happened."

THIRTEEN

Parents Can Help Lower the Risks of Teen Driving

PR Newswire

> The most common cause of death in teens aged fifteen to nineteen is car accidents. This statistic has not gone unnoticed, and many states have increased restrictions on teen drivers to try to prevent teen traffic deaths. Parents who pay attention to their teens' activities and who set rules may be a stronger prevention measure, however. Two studies published by *Pediatrics* in September 2009 support this concept. This viewpoint, a PR Newswire article, summarizes the studies, explaining which risky teen driving behaviors occur less often with involved parents and why.

Two recent studies reveal that teen crashes and risky driving behaviors such as cell phone use, failure to wear seat belts, and drinking and driving are strongly linked with the way teens and parents communicate and approach rules about safety. The results of the studies by The Children's Hospital of Philadelphia (CHOP) and State Farm® were published today [September 28, 2010] in the journal *Pediatrics*. . . .

The studies are based on the nationally-representative National Young Driver Survey of more than 5,500 teenagers. The first study shows that teens who said their parents set clear rules, paid attention to where they were going and whom they were with, and did so in a supportive way were:

- half as likely to crash;
- twice as likely to wear seat belts;
- 71 percent less likely to drive while intoxicated ;
- 30 percent less likely to use a cell phone while driving.

These findings are compared to teens who said their parents were less involved.

Parents can lessen incidences of dangerous driving by setting rules about where teens are allowed to drive and with whom they may ride.

Teens Are Ultimately Responsible for Their Behaviors

A second study found that teens who reported being the main driver of a vehicle were twice as likely to be involved in a crash, compared with teens who said they shared a vehicle with other family members. Nearly 75 percent of the teens surveyed reported being the main driver of a car.

"Once they're behind the wheel, teens have ultimate responsibility for their behavior" says Kenneth Ginsburg, MD, MS Ed, co-author of the study. "But kids who said their parents set rules in a supportive way were half as likely to crash compared with teens who saw their parents as less involved."

According to the researchers, there are specific things parents can do to keep teens safer around driving: set clear rules about driving; talk with kids about where they're going and who they're with; and make sure teens know the rules are in place because you care about them and their safety—not because you wish to control them. This approach may make it more likely teens will tell their parents what is going on in their lives. This in turn helps parents better follow through on the rules they set with their kids.

Approximately half of the teens surveyed reported that their parents consistently set rules, paid attention to where they were going and who they would be with in a way that was supportive.

"Our data show that one of the safest decisions families can make is for parents to control access to the keys for at least the first 6 to 12 months after a teen gets his license," says Flaura Koplin Winston, MD, PhD, study co-author and scientific director of the Center for Injury Research and Prevention at CHOP. "Our data show an alarming trend—almost three-quarters of teens say they have easy access to a car. Compared to teens who have to share a car, these teens are twice as likely to crash and more likely to speed and to use a cell phone while driving. When teens have to ask for the keys before taking the car, it naturally creates the opportunity for parents to have conversations with their teens about where they are going, who they will be with, and to review the house rules about driving with passengers, wearing seat belts, using cell phones, and which routes are safe."

"The first adult decision he's had to make is choosing between driving and texting."

Other research has found that a person's greatest lifetime chance of being in a fatal crash occurs during the first 6 to 12 months after receiving a license as a teenager. State Graduated Driver Licensing laws have been proven to reduce this risk by keeping new drivers out of the most dangerous situations during this crucial time. These findings confirm that parents who set rules are also effective in protecting their children from crashing.

Teens Need to Be Warned of the Risks of Playing the "Choking Game"

Paula Hunt

A risky, infrequently discussed teen behavior is sweep-
ing the country. An estimated sixty children and teens
die from it every year in the United States, although
that number may be much higher. Many children, teens,
and parents are not even aware of it—until their friend,
sibling, classmate, child, or neighbor dies. In this article
for *Current Health Teens*, writer Paula Hunt exposes the
"choking game." Hunt describes the risky "game," explains
why children and teens are attracted to it, and relates the
stories of several victims and what their families, friends,
and communities are doing to prevent more such tragedies.

Hey, want to try something that will give you a real head rush?
Make you feel dreamy and light-headed? C'mon, it's fun!
Maybe you've seen a video of the choking game on the Internet
or heard your friends talking about it. Kids try to make one another pass out on purpose by squeezing one another's necks. Or they
try it alone by putting their necks in homemade nooses and tying
them to doorknobs or bedposts.

Paula Hunt, "Strangle Hold: Intentional Choking Won't Just Leave You Breathless—It Could
Leave You Dead," *Current Health Teens*, vol. 37, no. 6, February 2011. Copyright © 2011 by
Scholastic Inc. All rights reserved. Reproduced by permission.

The buzz on the activity is just that: Doing it will give you a buzz, making you feel dizzy and tingly. Teens come up with many reasons to try it: Unlike using drugs, it's not illegal; unlike smoking cigarettes, it doesn't cause cancer; and unlike drinking alcohol, it doesn't cost money. Unless it costs a life, as it did for Daniel's friend.

Losing a Friend

Daniel had never heard of intentional choking until he was at a friend's house with another boy he didn't know. "We were really bored, and they said they wanted to play this game," says 16-year-old Daniel, who lives in Washington state. "At first I was kind of scared, but they kept bugging me, and I just gave in."

His friend choked him, and when Daniel woke up, he couldn't remember what had happened. "You're just dazed and confused," he says. Daniel tried it five times with friends after that; then he quit suddenly. What made him stop? One of his best friends died doing it.

"I didn't know how dangerous it was," says Daniel. "When I hear kids talking about the choking game now, I tell them to look at the facts. It can kill you."

Losing a Brother and a Son

There are no official statistics, but some experts believe that every year more than 60 kids and teens in the United States die of accidental suffocation they thought was going to give them a high. Maybe that doesn't sound like a lot to you—unless one of those 60 was your friend or a member of your family. Kelly T., a 14-year-old from Washington state knows what that's like. In March 2009, Kelly found her big brother, Kevin, unconscious and kneeling by his bed with the belt from a bathrobe tied around his neck.

Kelly thought he was kidding around at first. She started screaming Kevin, Kevin, stop doing that! and tried to untie the knot. It was too tight; she was too late. Fifteen-year-old Kevin T. died doing something he never thought would end his life.

Kids often fool around with choking behavior, but playing the choking "game" can end in death.

Kevin's best friend, Colton C., 17, says they used to talk about how stupid it was to take drugs and drink alcohol. He wishes Kevin had talked to him about self-suffocation. "Maybe I could have stopped him," says Colton. "I would have told him it's not worth it."

Michael G., 15, was also a friend of Kevin's. He had never heard of people choking themselves for fun until he learned that was how his buddy had died. "I was shocked," says Michael. "Kevin was such a fun and great guy; he's the last person I would have guessed would have tried something like that."

That's the thing about the risky pastime, which about three times as many boys as girls try. You can't predict who's going to play it—or die because of it. The victims are rich kids and poor kids, athletes and nerds, country kids and city kids.

Thirteen-year-old Colin R. was an honor student who was passionate about surfing and skateboarding, as well as playing soccer, cello, and guitar. His mom, Trish, says, "He was a happy, sweet, smart, awesome boy." But none of those qualities could save Colin in September 2005, when he was found hanging in the closet of his bedroom at his family's home in Washington state. Colin's mom is sure that he didn't want to die. She believes that in the confused state that happens right before someone passes out, he was unable to think straight and remove the noose.

Losing Your Life

Teens may not think that self-suffocation is dangerous. But they couldn't be more wrong. The object of the activity is to temporarily stop the flow of oxygen-rich blood, says Dr. Thomas Andrew, New Hampshire's chief medical examiner. He investigates deaths, such as those of suffocation victims. "The reason kids think there's a high is that a proper amount of oxygen isn't being delivered to [the] brain," he says. That can cause death in less than five minutes.

Most kids who try suffocation do it with friends, they take turns suffocating one another and laugh when someone passes out, has convulsions, or pees on himself or herself. But there's no safety in numbers when it comes to this activity. You may think your friends are looking out for you, but they can't keep your brain cells from being destroyed. Once brain cells die, they are not replaced. "It might look funny to see your friend lying on the ground jerking and twitching," says Andrew. "But a little bit of your friend dies

Choking-Game Deaths Compared with Suicides by Hanging or Suffocation

Shown below is the age distribution of US youths aged 6 to 19 years whose deaths were attributed to the "choking game" (82 instances) during 1995–2007, compared with youths whose deaths were attributed to suicide by hanging/suffocation (5,101 instances) during 1999–2005.

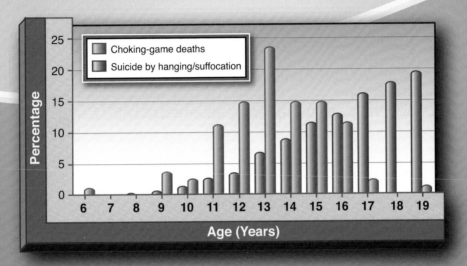

Taken from: Centers for Disease Control and Prevention, "Unintentional Strangulation Deaths from the 'Choking Game' Among Youths Aged 6–19 Years—United States, 1995–2007," *Morbidity and Mortality Weekly Report*, February 15, 2008. www.cdc.gov/mmwr/preview/mm570691.htm.

every time this happens." (Recently, some police departments have brought charges against teens who choked their friends for fun or taught the technique to others.)

Aside from death, there are big risks that come with choking yourself. You could fall, hit your head and suffer a concussion, scar your face, or lose a tooth or an eye. You could end up with permanent brain damage that leads to seizures and memory loss.

Levi Draher, 19, considers himself lucky to be alive. He spent three days in a coma and four days on life support in a Texas hospital after his mom found him unconscious with a rope around his neck in October 2006. He spent four months in physical therapy and speech therapy to get back to where he had been before the incident.

Today, Draher lives on his own. He has a driver's license and works full time but still suffers from permanent short-term memory loss. And his goal of flying airplanes is gone—the choking incident ended that dream forever.

"I could have been paralyzed or [become] a vegetable," says Draher. "I shouldn't have done it. Maybe other kids can look at me and say, 'It's not worth it.'"

A Fatal Mistake

Draher is one of the few kids to survive such a situation. For Kevin T., Colin R., and many others, however, it's too late.

"I miss him a lot," says Kevin's friend Michael. "He made a mistake, which we all do. The difference is he's not coming back. I hope other kids realize this isn't a game; it's a matter of life and death."

FIFTEEN

Warning Teens About the "Choking Game" May Just Promote It

Christina A. Samuels

When preventable, unexpected deaths of children and teens occur in a community, it would seem that the natural response of all educators would be to sound a loud warning. That is not what some families of "choking game" victims have discovered, reports Christina A. Samuels, a staff writer for *Education Week*. Samuels explains the "choking game" phenomenon and relates the difficulties encountered by some victims' parents when they have tried to share their stories with their children's classmates and parents. Some educators are afraid that telling children and teens about the phenomenon will increase, not decrease, the number of cases because, having learned about the "game," more young people will then try it.

Renée Mills knew something was happening to her bright, blue-eyed, 13-year-old son, Dakota, in the weeks before he died.

Too often, she said, the school nurse called home to say the 7th grader, known as Coty, was complaining about headaches. His temper was short. A former school nurse herself, Ms. Mills wondered whether her son was playing tricks on staff members at

Lunenburg Middle School, located in this rural community a little more than an hour southwest of Richmond, Va. But worried, she asked a family friend a few years older than Coty to gently probe to see whether her son might be using drugs.

On March 29, Coty Mills was found dead in his bedroom closet, with a device made of two belts wrapped around his neck.

Ms. Mills now believes her son's headaches, glazed eyes, and aggressiveness were indications that he was playing the "choking game," a practice in which people briefly cut off the flow of air and blood to their brains because of the temporary "rush" or euphoria they feel when oxygen and blood flow is restored.

A Spate of Teen Deaths

Such asphyxial activities are not new, but a spate of deaths like Coty's among young people around the country in the past year has brought further media attention to the subject and turned parents like Ms. Mills into advocates for greater awareness of the dangers involved.

But the subject is a sensitive one for schools. Some administrators have actively enlisted in efforts to inform students and parents about the risks of practices like the choking game, while other educators say they're worried that publicizing the subject among students risks inspiring copycat behavior.

"School districts in my neck of the woods say, 'Don't tell them, or they'll do it,' which to my belief is absurd," said Dr. Thomas A. Andrew, the chief medical examiner for the state of New Hampshire.

Dr. Andrew first learned about asphyxiation games in 2001, when he was asked to do an autopsy on a 13-year-old boy. He ruled the boy's death a suicide. Further investigation, and the death of a 12-year-old boy in a nearby town under similar circumstances, prompted him to change his ruling on that death to accidental.

Anecdotal Evidence Only

The number of minors in the United States who might be dying from asphyxial activities is completely anecdotal, with estimates ranging from fewer than 100 deaths per year to more than 500. Neither figure has any solid basis in data, experts warn, and little research on the subject exists.

Sometimes, such practices take place in groups, in which participants are able to revive each other if one loses consciousness. In some cases, participants hold their breath or hyperventilate to pass out; in others, they use some kind of ligature, such as a belt or cord, to choke off their air supply. Deaths occur most often when people engage in the practice alone, using a ligature.

Asphyxiation in conjunction with masturbation has been a cause of such deaths, most commonly among young adult males. Pamela C. Cantor, a lecturer in psychology at the Harvard Medical School and a past president of the American Association of Suicidology, said she first encountered descriptions of what is known as autoerotic asphyxiation in the 1960s.

"My guess is that this is some kind of sexual activity," Ms. Cantor said of recent deaths attributed to the choking game. She lectures in schools and to groups across the country about recognition and prevention of risky adolescent behavior.

Others say the choking game—also known by such names as space monkey, gasper, choke out, and cloud nine—appears to have no sexual intent among many young people.

"For most of the young people to [whom] I have spoken, it's about getting a high and not more than that," said Dr. Joseph R. Zanga, a Greenville, N.C., pediatrician and a past president of the American Academy of Pediatricians.

Fear of Copycatting

Since Coty Mills' death, Ms. Mills has become a crusader in her community, trying to get the word out to the 1,700-student Lunenburg district that the choking game has fatal consequences. But while the community has embraced her, she believes a few people are still not ready to listen to her message.

"People are afraid for you to speak because they're afraid you're going to have copycatting," Ms. Mills said one day last month [May 2006] a few hours after addressing a group of about

Some educators are afraid that discussing the choking game with teens may lead them to try it.

45 people gathered at the same middle school her son attended. Though the district allowed her to use the school as a gathering place, it declined to send fliers about the event home with the students.

"They're afraid that some kid is going to go home and try it," said Ms. Mills, who was so determined that youths in her community see the dangers of the "game" that she insisted her son's casket be left open. Hundreds of people attended his funeral.

Wayne Staples, the superintendent of the Lunenburg district, said his system does not send any notices home with students that aren't directly school-related. He attended Ms. Mills' May 10 presentation, and said he thought she did a good job explaining that asphyxiation "games" can take place without parents being aware.

"I wish there had been more people there," Mr. Staples said of the event.

The 15,000-student Springfield, Ill., district has also wrestled with how to deal with the subject.

"I'm truthful when I say I'm really agonizing over this," said Robin M. Yoggerst, a student-support leader in the district, where an 11-year-old died in June 2005 from an accidental asphyxiation that some believe resulted from the choking game.

While she said the subject is appropriate to raise with adults, administrators are more wary of talking to students about it.

"It's not like we want to glamorize anything," Ms. Yoggerst said.

Outreach Efforts

Kate Blake, whose 11-year-old son, Dylan, died last October when he looped a belt around his neck and attached the other end to his bunk bed, said the superintendent of the 14,600-student St. Johns County, Fla., district, Joseph Joyner, was receptive to her request that information about asphyxial activities be widely publicized among parents. The principal of her son's school, she believes, was less so.

"At the lower level, they just don't want to deal with it," said Ms. Blake, who lives in St. Augustine, Fla., and has created an extensive Web site to disseminate information about the choking game, dylan-the-boy-blake.com. "More often than not, the response I get is, 'We don't want to plant the seed.'"

David D. Baker, the superintendent of the 4,700-student Springboro, Ohio, district, has heard some of that grumbling. He heard about the choking game, then got reports that a group of 3rd graders in his district were playing a game to see who could hold their breath the longest.

Administrators brought the children together in January and told them the practice was dangerous. Then, Mr. Baker sent a letter to parents explaining the dangers of asphyxial activities. Administrators also gathered the school's entire 3rd grade class for an assembly to warn them about the game.

"We had some parents upset with me," Mr. Baker said. "They thought that I was accusing their children."

But from Mr. Baker's perspective, he was trying to reach out to students before anyone got hurt. "I'll never know how many kids were saved because we put it out there," Mr. Baker said of the outreach effort.

From the perspective of health professionals, alerting parents about the specific dangers of the choking game is a good approach. For students, general warnings about the activity can be incorporated into lessons about other risky behaviors, they say.

Asphyxial activities should be addressed the same way as behaviors such as smoking and "huffing," or inhaling chemicals to get high, said Dr. Andrew, the New Hampshire medical examiner. "The same administrators probably wouldn't object to a flier about smoking," he said, "so why would they object to this?"

Dangers Must Be Communicated

Ms. Blake, the Florida mother who lost a son, said schools must acknowledge that the activities are happening and talk to parents about them, along with other risky youth behaviors, such as drug use.

"That's the easiest and most resourceful way to do it," Ms. Blake said. "My mission is, I don't want to reinvent the wheel. I just want to add a spoke."

In districts where students have died from asphyxial practices, administrators say they tried to address the problem comprehensively: warning parents, while reminding students that they need to tell trusted adults if they hear about or see their classmates engaging in such behaviors.

Ann E. Shortt, the superintendent of the 14,500-student Fairbanks North Star Borough district in Fairbanks, Alaska,

Warning Signs That a Person Is Playing the Choking Game

You may observe any of the following signs if a friend is playing the choking game:

- Discussion of the game or its aliases

- Bloodshot eyes

- Marks on the neck

- Wearing high-necked shirts, even in warm weather

- Frequent, severe headaches

- Disorientation after spending time alone

- Increased and uncharacteristic irritability or hostility

- Ropes, scarves, and belts tied to bedroom furniture or doorknob or found knotted on the floor

- The unexplained presence of dog leashes, choke collars, bungee cords, etc.

- Petechiae (pinpoint bleeding spots) under the skin of the face, especially the eyelids, or the conjunctiva (the lining of the eyelids and eyes)

Taken from: Centers for Disease Control and Prevention, Injury Prevention & Control, "The Choking Game: CDC's Findings on a Risky Youth Behavior," February 15, 2008. www.cdc.gov/homeandrecreationalsafety/Choking/choking_game.html.

said her district sent letters home to all parents after 13-year-old Andrew Freeman died from what was believed to be the choking game on March 29, the same day as Coty Mills.

In addition, the district plans two "safety summits" for parents that will focus on asphyxial activities, as well as on Internet safety and bullying. The district is also reaching out to community groups such as churches.

"Our philosophy is to communicate as much as we can with parents, as quickly as we have accurate information," Ms. Shortt said. In this case, as in many others, the parents were advocates for getting the word out to the community.

"They were so supportive of us," Ms. Shortt said. "Very open."

SIXTEEN

Extreme Sports Can Provide Lifetime Health Benefits for Teens

Nichole Buswell

> Motocross, snowboarding, skateboarding, and other so-called extreme or action sports have been growing in popularity—along with injuries from these risky sports. In this viewpoint, writer Nichole Buswell explains their popularity, how the risks can be lessened, and what researchers have learned that might convince the parents of teens that in the long run the benefits of extreme sports may outweigh the risks.

For a growing number of teens, nothing beats the thrill of pulling off new tricks in action sports such as skateboarding, snowboarding, and bicycle motocross (BMX). "I love the jumps and the weightless feeling you get when you're in the air," says Greg D., a 16-year-old from Pennsylvania who is a member of his school's popular ski and snowboard club. But while action sports may take fun to new levels, they also involve a set of heightened risks—and deserve serious thought.

Nichole Buswell, "Flying High: Grinds and Space Walks, Backflips and Front Flips. Landing a 180 on the Half-Pipe," *Current Health Teens*, vol. 37, no. 3, November 2010, pp. 16–19. Copyright © 2010 by Scholastic Inc. All rights reserved. Reproduced by permission.

High-Stakes Sports

Now more than ever, recognition of action sports is soaring. Snowboarding and skateboarding are among the fastest-growing sports nationally, according to an American Sports Data survey, with three of five U.S. kids and teens saying they watch action sports on TV. But as the popularity of action sports has increased, so has the number of injuries among young participants, according to the American Academy of Orthopaedic Surgeons (AAOS). "Many teens don't realize the rigorous training required of extreme sports athletes," says Dr. George Russell, spokesperson for the AAOS. He notes that athletes who compete in the X Games and Olympics spend years working their way up to the gravity-defying stunts they perform on TV.

There is good reason for that practice and preparation. Unlike traditional sports such as basketball and soccer, action sports often propel athletes high in the air. That leaves them more prone to falls that can lead to serious injuries—something top American snowboarder Kevin Pearce experienced firsthand. When he failed to land a twisting double backflip during a trial for the 2010 Winter Olympics, Pearce suffered a traumatic brain injury. Though he was wearing a helmet at the time, the accident left him hospitalized in critical condition. Fortunately, Pearce has regained his ability to walk and talk and is on a slow but steady road to recovery.

Though extreme, Pearce's injury is not uncommon. Snowboarding causes more injuries than any other outdoor activity, notes the Centers for Disease Control and Prevention, with about half of those injured between the ages of 10 and 24. And snowboarding is not the only culprit: The majority of sports-related head injuries occur during bicycling, skateboarding, or skating, according to the American Academy of Pediatrics and Safe Kids USA.

Though head injuries can be the most devastating, other types of injuries are common in action sports. Those include damage to the knees, as well as broken wrists and elbows, notes Russell. Sometimes, injuries are severe enough to harm growth plates—areas at the ends of long bones that are the weakest parts of teens'

Extreme sports snowboarder Kevin Pearce (pictured) suffered a traumatic brain injury during the 2010 Winter Olympic trials. Although snowboarding is responsible for more injuries than any other outdoor activity, some experts say that action sports can help teens stay fit throughout their lifetimes.

growing skeletons. "These types of injuries generally require surgery and can lead to stunted growth or even deformities," warns Russell.

Blame It on Your Brain

If action sports are so dangerous, why are so many teens drawn to them? The answer may be in your brain, says Tara Kuther, a psychology professor at Western Connecticut State University. She notes that teens' brain chemistry makes them more likely to be drawn to activities that involve a degree of risk. During adolescence, Kuther explains, the parts of the brain responsible for strong emotion develop very quickly. At the same time, the parts that handle judgment and logical thinking lag behind—leaving many teens hard-pressed to control their impulses. When it comes to attempting risky moves in action sports, teens may quite literally forget to look before they leap.

The brain changes during adolescence cause the emotional "high" which often accompanies risky activity to be particularly strong, Kuther adds. That means that the danger of wiping out during a trick may be the very reason a teen feels compelled to try it in the first place. (Thus the popularity of MTV's bone-crunching stunt show *Scarred*, which airs footage of spectacular wipeouts—and the often-gruesome aftermath.)

Reducing Your Risk

So how can you prevent impulse from leading to injury? Try taking a time-out. Think carefully about the benefits and risks, and "then pause before jumping into an activity," Kuther advises. If you are uncomfortable with trying a sport or a trick but don't want to lose out on time with friends, just hang out and watch the action.

If you choose to get in the game, the right safety equipment is a must. Since 2009, the Winter X Games have required helmets for all competitors—a trend that is catching on nationwide. Helmet use among skiers and snowboarders has risen 19 percent since 2008, according to a survey by the National Ski Areas Association. "My friends and I always wear our helmets when we go [snowboarding]," says Greg. For skateboarders and bikers, helmet use can reduce the risk of head injury by 85 percent, according to Safe Kids USA.

Equally important in avoiding injury is being honest with yourself about your own skills. Greg and his buddies "look out for each other and don't try tricks that are past our ability level," he says. For novice snowboarders, that might mean sticking with beginner slopes until you're comfortable taking on steeper ones or advancing to the half-pipe. In skateboarding, instructor Sean Nguyen recommends first mastering the basics of balance, turns, and stops before trying grinds, slides, and basic tricks.

No matter the sport, it's best to begin under the guidance of an instructor who knows the ropes. One recent study of injured snowboarders found that 88 percent hadn't taken lessons. "A skilled instructor will not only provide technical instructions but will also instill confidence," says Nguyen.

The Action Sports Advantage

Though they can be more dangerous than traditional sports, action sports may actually have an edge in terms of helping teens stay fit throughout their lives. Researchers at Johns Hopkins University in Baltimore found that for a young person who biked or skateboarded more than four times a week, the chance of becoming an overweight adult fell by 48 percent. Meanwhile, for those who played soccer or other more traditional sports, the odds of being overweight later in life dropped by only 20 percent.

Greg prefers snowboarding to traditional team sports for several reasons. "I like that I can go at my own pace. I take a break when I want to or push myself when I want to. Also, it's not as structured [as organized sports], and it is noncompetitive." Though action sports carry their own set of risks, there's no denying their appeal. As long as teens take the right safety precautions, action sports can be a great way to have fun—and keep in shape for years to come.

What You Should Know About Risky Teen Behavior

Preventable Teen Deaths

According to the US National Center for Health Statistics (NCHS) in 2009 the five most prevalent causes of teen deaths were:

- accidents (unintentional injuries)—48 percent;
- homicide—13 percent;
- suicide—11 percent;
- cancer—6 percent; and
- heart disease—3 percent.

Teens and Motor Vehicle Accidents

According to the NCHS, in 2009 48 percent of teens died in accidents, and 73 percent of those were motor vehicle accidents—overall more than 30 percent of total teen fatalities. The rest of the 48 percent of teens who died from unintentional injuries in 2009 were killed in the following ways:

- unintentional poisoning—7 percent;
- unintentional drowning—5 percent;
- other land-transport accidents—3 percent;
- unintentional discharge of a firearm—2 percent; and
- other unintentional deaths—10 percent.

Drug and Alcohol Use Among Teens

According to an April 6, 2011, CBS News story on teen substance abuse:

- 10 percent use ecstasy;
- 40 percent use pot;
- 71 percent have had their first drink of alcohol before graduating high school; and
- 25 percent have had their first drink by age twelve.

According to the Centers for Disease Control and Prevention (CDC), 28 percent of teens reported riding in a car with a driver who had been drinking, and 10 percent of teens had driven a car while intoxicated.

Teens and Text Messaging

According to a 2009 survey of teenagers by The National Campaign to Prevent Teen and Unplanned Pregnancy:

- 20 percent of teens have sent nude or seminude pictures or videos of themselves;
- 39 percent of teens have engaged in sexually suggestive messaging; and
- nearly 40 percent of teens are aware of sexy pictures and posts being forwarded to others than the originally intended recipient.

The National Highway Traffic Safety Administration reports that nearly one in five traffic fatalities involves a distracted driver.

A 2009 Pew Research study on teens who text while driving found that

- 33 percent of sixteen- to seventeen-year-old drivers report sending and reading text messages while driving; and
- nearly half of all teens have been passengers in vehicles where a driver has been texting.

Teens and Sexually Transmitted Infections (STIs)

According to the CDC, STIs are a serious public health problem in the United States, and most STIs are disproportionately common among young people:

- Every year 19 million new cases of HIV and other STIs are reported in the United States; almost half of them are in teens and young people aged fifteen to twenty-four.
- Chlamydia is reported to be four times more prevalent in fifteen- to twenty-four-year olds than in the general population (aged ten to sixty-five).
- Gonorrhea is reported to be four times more prevalent in fifteen- to twenty-four-year olds than in the general population (aged ten to sixty-five).
- An estimated 5,259 youth aged thirteen to twenty-four contracted HIV/AIDS in the thirty-three states that reported to the CDC. This represents about 14 percent of all HIV/AIDS cases reported, according to 2006 data.

Other Risks to Teens

The following statistics, as reported by the CDC, might not make as many headlines as those mentioned above; nevertheless, they represent serious risks:

- 12 percent of teens are obese, making them more susceptible to other serious health conditions like type 2 diabetes, high blood pressure, and heart disease.
- 19 percent of teens are smokers, 14 percent smoke cigars, and 9 percent use smokeless tobacco, putting them at risk for contracting lung cancer, oral cancers, and emphysema in the future.
- 10 percent of teens do not wear seatbelts when riding in a vehicle.
- 85 percent of teens do not wear bicycle helmets when riding their bicycles.

What You Should Do About Risky Teen Behavior

Being a teenager means trying new things, testing your independence, and having to make more—as well as more important—decisions on your own. The upside of this is the thrill of new things, new friends, and new freedoms. The downside is the tendency to sometimes make decisions to take risks that are exciting at the time but have devastating long-term effects. Although no one gets through this period of life mistake-free, you can be proactive by understanding why teens have a propensity to take risks, knowing the importance of making good friends, and by raising your voice to help others in potentially risky situations.

Understand Your Brain

Scientists are learning more every year about the way the human brain develops. The brain changes tremendously during the teen years and does not finish growing until early adulthood. Much attention has been given to the immaturity and the growth that take place in the frontal lobe during adolescence when, quite literally, the decision-making and impulse-controlling sections of the brain are being developed. Just knowing that your brain is still developing while you are a teen is important because understanding what you are up against will remind you to think twice—or three times—before making decisions.

Understanding your brain is also important for another reason: The actions that you take while you are a teenager—and your brain is still growing—will permanently affect how your brain turns out. For example, enough alcohol will permanently damage the brain no matter your age, but it will more severely devastate a teen brain. Repeated studies have supported the fact that alcohol actually impairs the learning ability of teens—perhaps permanently. The teen brain is also more susceptible to all kinds of addiction. Not only are teens more likely than adults to become dependent on alcohol, tobacco, and drugs in the first place, but addictions that begin as a teen are far more difficult to overcome.

Make Good Friends

Any developmental psychologist would agree that a normal part of being a teenager is pulling away from your parents—and closer to your friends. It is an important part of growing up and becoming an independent person.

Friends are so important during these years that when friends—or people that you want to be your friends—are around, the allure of taking risks is stronger. Research released in January 2011 by Temple University neuroscientists explains why. The study looked at brain activity while subjects participated in a video game where if they drove somewhere more quickly they would get more money. In the game, running a yellow light might get them to their destination faster, but it also increased the risk of an accident and a longer delay. If teens had their friends sitting with them, they were significantly more likely to take dangerous risks than if alone.

Using functional magnetic resonance imaging, the scientists discovered why teens are more likely to take risks with friends around. When teens were with their friends during risky decisions, the reward centers of their brains were more active. In other words, it is not that having your friends with you makes you less intelligent but rather that having your friends with you makes taking risks more exciting and more attractive. The risk-taking decisions of adults in the same study were not affected by the presence of friends.

Because friends are—in general—so influential during the teen years, it is crucial that you surround yourself with *good* friends who have your best interests at heart. In the study, *just the presence* of friends made risky behavior more attractive. Imagine what your brain is going to do if your friends are *overtly pressuring* you to take dangerous risks. Running a red light, experimenting with drugs, or trying something like the choking game or "drifting" might suddenly sound like a good idea. Decisions made in the moment—like texting a revealing picture of yourself—often have devastating consequences.

Raise Your Voice

In light of this science, being a good friend is probably the single most important thing that you can to do prevent risky teen behavior. Understand that simply your presence and also your actions and words impact the other teens that you are with, especially your friends. Be the one to wear your seatbelt and to nag your friends to do the same. Be the one to make the party fun without drugs or alcohol or to find something else to do altogether if you know that alcohol will be the focus of the party. Do not encourage your friends to do something that they might regret later or that you know to be against their beliefs. Tell your friends if you think they are doing something dangerous.

You can also raise your voice by being active at your school and in your community. Risky teen behavior encompasses a number of issues: drugs, alcohol, driving, sex, the choking game, and more. There are nonprofit organizations dedicated to each one, and many such as Students Against Destructive Decisions (SADD) will help students start local chapters at their schools or in their communities to create discussion and raise awareness of issues in hopes of preventing risky behaviors and their tragic consequences.

If starting a local chapter of SADD sounds too daunting, you can raise your voice in other ways. For example the National Campaign to Prevent Teen Pregnancy sponsors a National Day to Prevent Teen Pregnancy every year. Check it out on its website, talk to your teachers or school counselors, and ask your school to participate, and offer to volunteer. You can also just participate yourself by taking part in their National Day Quiz online and sending a link to the quiz to your friends or posting it on Facebook or Twitter.

Being a positive force in your school and community is by no means without risks. You may at first feel uncomfortable vocalizing disapproval of a friend's choices or being a part of an organization that may stigmatize you in the eyes of other classmates. But this type of risk is one that will perhaps define who you are and what you stand for and is a risk you can ultimately feel good about.

The editors have compiled the following list of organizations concerned with the issues presented in this book. The descriptions are derived from materials provided by the organizations. All have publications or information available for interested readers. The list was compiled on the date of publication of the present volume; the information provided here may change. Be aware that many organizations take several weeks or longer to respond to inquiries, so allow as much time as possible.

Advocates for Youth
2000 M St. NW, Ste. 750, Washington, DC 20036
(202) 419-3420 • fax: (202) 419-1448
e-mail: information@advocatesforyouth.org
website: www.advocatesforyouth.org

Advocates for Youth creates programs and advocates for policies that help people make informed and responsible decisions about their reproductive and sexual health. The group also offers information, training, and strategic assistance to organizations, policy makers, youth activists, and the media in the United States and the developing world.

Centers for Disease Control and Prevention (CDC)
Division of Adolescent and School Health
4770 Buford Hwy. NE, MS K29, Atlanta, GA 30341
(800) 232-4636
e-mail: www.cdc.gov/healthyyouth/yrbs/contactyrbs.htm
website: www.cdc.gov/healthyyouth

The CDC is one of the major components of the US Department of Health and Human Services. Every other year the CDC Division of Adolescent and School Health conducts the *Youth*

Risk Behavior Survey (YRBS). The full report and many other publications presenting information from the *YRBS* are available at the CDC's Healthy Youth website as well as "Youth Online" an interactive tool that produces custom graphs and tables.

Family Research Council (FRC)
801 G St. NW, Washington, DC 20001
(202) 393-2100 • fax: (202) 393-2134
website: www.frc.org

The FRC develops public policy that upholds the institutions of marriage and family. Among the issues it supports is abstinence-only education. Publications on AIDS and abstinence-only education are available on the website, including "Why Wait: The Benefits of Abstinence Until Marriage."

Games Adolescents Shouldn't Play (GASP)
W321 N7669 Silverspring Ln., Hartland, WI 53029
e-mail: contact@gaspinfo.com

GASP is a volunteer organization founded with the goal of ending the choking game, an asphyxiation activity that too often ends in unintentional death. GASP partners with other organizations that include choking game education as part of their overall message. It provides free downloadable educational materials—brochures, PowerPoint presentations, and videos.

Girlshealth.gov
8270 Willow Oaks Corporate Dr., Ste. 301, Fairfax, VA 22031
website: www.girlshealth.gov

The mission of the Girlshealth.gov website, developed by the Office on Women's Health in the Department of Health and Human Services, is to promote healthy, positive behaviors in girls between the ages of ten and sixteen. The site gives girls reliable, useful information on the health issues they will face as they become young women and tips on handling relationships with family and friends, at school and at home.

The Heritage Foundation
214 Massachusetts Ave. NE, Washington, DC 20002-4999
(202) 546-4000 • fax: (202) 546-8328
e-mail: info@heritage.org • website: www.heritage.org

The Heritage Foundation is a conservative think tank that has published numerous articles and papers on sex education, particularly the effectiveness of abstinence-only education and virginity pledges.

The National Campaign to Prevent Teen Pregnancy
1776 Massachusetts Ave. NW, Ste. 200, Washington, DC 20036
(202) 478-8500
e-mail: campaign@thenc.org • website: www.teenpregnancy.org

The goal of The National Campaign to Prevent Teen Pregnancy is to prevent teen pregnancy by supporting values and stimulating actions that are consistent with a pregnancy-free adolescence. The organization publishes reports and fact sheets on teen attitudes, behaviors, and contraceptive use, including *Where and When Teens First Have Sex* and *The Sexual Behavior of Young Adolescents*.

National Council on Alcoholism and
Drug Dependence (NCADD)
244 E. Fifty-Eighth St., 4th Fl., New York, NY 10022
(212) 269-7797
e-mail: national@ncadd.org • website: www.ncadd.org

In addition to helping individuals overcome addictions, NCADD advises the federal government on drug and alcohol policies and develops substance abuse prevention and education programs for youth. It publishes fact sheets and pamphlets on substance abuse, including, *What Can You Do About Someone Else's Drinking?* and *Who's Got the Power? You . . . or Drugs?*

National Eating Disorders Association (NEDA)
603 Stewart St., Ste. 803, Seattle, WA 98101
(206) 382-3587 • toll-free: (800) 931-2237
e-mail: info@nationaleatingdisorders.org
website: www.nationaleatingdisorders.org

NEDA is the largest not-for-profit organization in the United States working to prevent eating disorders and to provide treatment referrals to those suffering from anorexia, bulimia, and binge-eating disorder and those concerned with body image and weight issues. Its website offers various resources for parents, educators, and coaches for dealing with these issues among teens.

National Highway Traffic Safety Administration (NHTSA)
1200 New Jersey Ave. SE, West Bldg., Washington, DC 20590
(888) 327-4236
e-mail: www.nhtsa.gov/nhtsa-dpmextn/jsp/email/email_page.jsp
website: www.nhtsa.gov

The NHTSA directs highway traffic safety programs mandated by federal laws to prevent vehicular crashes and their tragic personal and financial consequences. It provides grants for state and local safety programs, sets and enforces vehicle safety performance standards, and conducts vehicle and traffic safety research, which is made available through several databases at their website.

Planned Parenthood Federation of America
434 W. Thirty-Third St., New York, NY 10001
(212) 541-7800 • fax: (212) 245-1845
e-mail: communications@ppfa.org
website: www.plannedparenthood.org

Planned Parenthood is an organization of affiliated health centers across the country that provides high-quality, affordable reproductive health care and sexual health information to more than 5 million people every year. It also publishes *Choice!*, a magazine that promotes activism on matters of reproductive choice.

Project Reality
1701 E. Lake Ave., Glenview, IL 60025
(847) 729-3298 • fax: (847) 729-9744
website: www.projectreality.org

Project Reality is an organization that develops educational programs that teach the benefits of abstinence from sexual activity as well as from the use of alcohol, drugs, and tobacco. Curricula and promotional items are available on its website.

Sexuality Information and Education Council of the United States (SIECUS)
130 W. Forty-Second St., Ste. 350, New York, NY 10036-7802
(212) 819-9770 • fax: (212) 819-9776
e-mail: siecus@siecus.org • website: www.siecus.org

SIECUS is an organization that provides information for parents, health professionals, educators, and communities in order to ensure that everybody receives comprehensive information about sexuality. It also works to have sound public policy developed on sexuality-related issues. The council publishes the quarterly journal *SIECUS Report*, fact sheets, and newsletters.

Students Against Destructive Decisions (SADD)
SADD National
255 Main St., Marlborough, MA 01752
(877) SAD-DINC • fax: (508) 481-5759
e-mail: info@sadd.org • website: www.sadd.org

What began in 1981 as Students Against Drunk Driving has now morphed into Students Against Destructive Decisions. The mission of this peer-to-peer activism organization is to provide students with the best prevention tools possible to deal with the issues of underage drinking, other drug use, risky and impaired driving, and other destructive decisions. SADD provides numerous resources, including statistics, information on how to start a SADD chapter at your school, a press release template, and fundraising ideas.

BIBLIOGRAPHY

Books

Lisa Bakewell, *Alcohol Information for Teens*. Detroit: Omnigraphics, 2009.

Dale Bick Carlson, Hannah Carlson, and Carol Nicklaus, *Are You Human or What? Teen Psychological Evolution*. Madison, CT: Bick, 2008.

John DiConsiglio, *True Confessions: Real Stories About Drinking and Drugs*. New York: Franklin Watts, 2008.

Joan Esherick, *The Silent Cry: Teen Suicide and Self-Destructive Behaviors*. Philadelphia: Mason Crest, 2005.

Ann McIntosh Hoffelder and Robert L. Hoffelder, *How the Brain Grows*. New York: Chelsea House, 2006.

Judith Horstman, *The "Scientific American" Day in the Life of Your Brain*. San Francisco: Jossey-Bass, 2009.

Bob Hugel, *I Did It Without Thinking: True Stories About Impulsive Decisions That Changed Lives*. New York: Franklin Watts, 2008.

Institute of Medicine and National Research Council Committee on the Science of Adolescence, *The Science of Adolescent Risk-Taking: Workshop Report*. Washington DC: National Academies Press, 2011. (Book available online at www.ncbi.nlm.nih.gov /books/NBK53418.)

Elizabeth Magill, *Drug Information for Teens*. Detroit: Omnigraphics, 2011.

Sherre Florence Phillips, *The Teen Brain*. New York: Chelsea House, 2007.

Michael Ungar, *Too Safe for Their Own Good: How Risk and Responsibility Helps Teens Thrive*. Crows Nest, NSW, Australia: Allen & Unwin, 2008.

Annie Winston, *A Father's Sexting Teen: The Brian Hunt Story.* Irvine, CA: Tri-Net, 2010.

Periodicals and Internet Sources

Garry Boulard, "Driving Under Experienced," *State Legislatures*, June 2006.

Jane D. Brown, Sarah Keller, and Susannah Stern, "Sex, Sexuality, Sexting, and Sex Ed: Adolescents and the Media," *Prevention Researcher*, November 2009.

Michael Cart, "A Literature of Risk: Teens Dealing with Violence and Other Risky Behaviors Can Get Help from Young Adult Fiction," *American Libraries*, October 8, 2010.

Centers for Disease Control and Prevention, "CDC Report Finds Gay, Lesbian and Bisexual Students at Greater Risk for Unhealthy, Unsafe Behaviors," June 6, 2011. www.cdc.gov /media/releases/2011/p0606_yrbsurvey.html.

Nancy Cook, "Young and Riskless," *Newsweek*, September 13, 2010.

Shannon P. Duffy, "Student's Privacy Rights Violated in Sexting, ACLU Suit Says," *Legal Intelligencer*, April 2, 2011.

Karina Hamalainen, "Your Teenage Brain: Adolescence Can Be a Turbulent Time. Find Out Why It's Largely Your Brain's Fault," *Science World*, November 9, 2009.

Sharon Jayson, "Expert: Risky Teen Behavior Is All in the Brain," *USA Today*, April 5, 2007.

———, "Report on Teen Risk Finds Hispanics Lacking," *USA Today*, June 5, 2008.

Kate Lunau, "Teenagers Wired to Take Risks: What's Difficult for Parents to Sort Out Is What Is Normal Behaviour and What's Cause for Real Concern," *Maclean's*, April 11, 2011.

Tracey Middlekauff, "Risky Business: For Most Teens, Making Risky Decisions Comes Naturally," *Current Health 2: A Weekly Reader Publication*, March 2009.

Kimberly Mitchell, "Remaining Safe and Avoiding Dangers Online," *Prevention Researcher*, December 2010.

Morbidity and Mortality Weekly Report, "Unintentional Strangulation Deaths from 'the Choking Game' Among Youths Aged 6–19 Years—United States, 1995–2007," February 15, 2008.

National Campaign to Prevent Teen and Unplanned Pregnancy and Cosmogirl.com, "Sex and Tech: Results from a Survey of Teens and Young Adults," 2008. www.thenationalcampaign.org /sextech/pdf/sextech_summary.pdf.

Lan Neugent and Tammy M. McGraw, "Sexting: Implications for Schools," Virginia Department of Education Division of Technology & Career Education, Office of Educational Technology *Information Brief,* October 2009. www.doe.virginia .gov/support/technology/info_briefs/sexting.pdf.

Tara Parker-Pope, "Digital Flirting: Easy to Do and Easy to Get Caught," *New York Times,* June 14, 2011.

Karen S. Peterson, "Three Factors Threaten Teens: Too Much Money, Boredom and Stress Can Lead to Substance Abuse," Special Reprint from *USA Today,* 2003. www.usatoday.com /educate/ondcp/lessons/Activity2.pdf.

Denise Rinaldo, "The Brain Game: Teens' Brains Are Complex and Fascinating. Find Out Why You Sometimes Make Bad Decisions and How You Can Train Your Brain to Make Good Ones," *Scholastic Choices,* February/March 2006.

Laurence Steinberg, "Risk Taking in Adolescence: New Perspectives from Brain and Behavioral Science," *Current Directions in Psychological Science,* vol. 16, no. 2, 2007.

INDEX